Recognition Garnered by the Book

Dear Mridul,

I am very impressed by your profile, by your deep knowledge on the subject, and the dedication you are showing at such a young age, God bless you.

I am pretty sure, one day your parents and your school would be proud of you.

Keep going, all the very best.

Dr AJAY K. DEWAN
M.D. (Medicine), FICA, FIMSA
Consultant Physician-Internal Medince
Diabotology, Cardiology

I have known Mridul since he was a child 2/3 years old. He was a child prodigy. He could recite the Hanuman Chalisa when he was hardly 3 years old flawlessly and I owned Aastha TV channel in those days. We would seek his Mother Madhuji's permission to shoot him on video and run his shows on the channel. The recitals were amazing and inspired awe and appreciation for his perfection. He grew up to have phenomenal abilities of memory and could perform feats of amazing memory by being able to remember the pages and lines of paragraphs in large books of 1000 pages. He performed an ability to read books with the books being closed or keeping eyes closed/blindfolded and read with his finger running over the text. He has grown up to be a fine man and I am sure his book will be a fantastic read and provide guidance and essential knowledge and understanding on the issue of weight loss, a desperate need of Millions of obese people the world over. I have no hesitation in recommending the book not only to the unhealthy but also to the healthy as it will bring to light astounding research and facts which will help in adding value to people's lives. My blessings again and best wishes for success to this best-seller which will top charts for a long, long time.

Mr. Kirit C. Mehta-Founder and ex-CMD AASTHA TV CHANNELS WORLDWIDE ..Now FOUNDER of ENRICH TV OTT PLATFORM dedicated to Coaching Mentoring & Motivation, launching Q3, 2020.

Incredible! At this tender age when children are fond of partying and enjoying themselves, Mridul has come up with this book which highlights the common physical problems of his generation and also has documented the solutions for them. He has emphasized the need of physical fitness, immunity boosting, mental agility for a healthy and stress free life which shows his awareness and sensitiveness towards the society. Remarkable!

Wishing him all the best for the future.

Regards

Mr. Mukesh K. Sharma

Dy. Registrar

Netaji Subhas University of Technology

Dwarka

NEW DELHI

Congratulations for having compiled some wonderful work. God bless you.

Principal, K.R. Mangalam World School,

Vikas Puri,

New Delhi.

The book is constructed on the memories and experiences of a young boy who aspires to share his fitness journey. The book works at two levels, first it motivates one to adopt a healthy lifestyle and second, provides the science involved into choosing healthy food.

The narrator doesn't just talk about food and health but provides logical and informative facts on energy balance, self-control techniques and the importance of time. Examples from day to day life are picked and answered in the most rational manner. Bits and pieces are joined together to give reader a realistically achievable plan towards a healthy lifestyle. The personal touch in the book makes it a relatable reading. Written in a transparent language with so much enthusiasm; this book should be read by people of all ages.

MAHENDER KUMAR

GM (ENGG)

AIR INDIA

NR

"I think Mridul could be one of the youngest ambassadors for health! At such a young age, he has given above-his-age insights and an ingenious, researched plan for weight loss and health. The book's language is easy to flow with and it is for all, irrespective of age. Health is a daunting question in the epidemic infested world these days. And, this book helps you maintain it with no pricey equipment or products. I see a bright future for him. Best wishes to Mridul and his family.

Prof. Samsher,

Professor, Department of Mechanical Engineering

Delhi Technological University, Delhi

The book written by Mr. Mridul Sharma is a gift to those who want to maintain their mind, body and soul. The book has very good suggestions to maintain a body in good health which is a source of good positive thoughts, energy and self environment. I wish Mr. Mridul Sharma all the success in future.

With kind regards,

Prof. Vijander Singh

Professor, Instrumentation and Control Engineering Department

Dean Student Welfare,

Netaji Subhas University of Technology,

Sec-3, Dwarka, New Delhi-110078

Dear Mridul,

Congratulations for your hard work and dedication which has reflected in the form of this book.

I really appreciate the efforts and energy put into it.

I wish you all success in your future endeavors. Keep up the good work.

Capt. Shailender kumar Narula

Air India

भारतीय प्रौद्योगिकी संस्थान रुड़की
वित्त एवं लेखा कार्यालय
रुड़की – 247 667, उत्तराखण्ड, भारत

INDIAN INSTITUTE OF TECHNOLOGY ROORKEE
FINANCE & ACCOUNTS OFFICE
ROORKEE - 247 667, (UTTARAKHAND), INDIA

TEL : +91 - 1332 - 285789 (O), 286789 (R) FAX : 01332 - 285822, 273560
e-mail : rastogi.gk@iitr.ac.in Web. : www.iitr.ac.in

जी० के० रस्तोगी
संयुक्त कुलसचिव (वित्त एवं लेखा)
G. K. Rastogi
Joint Registrar (Finance & Accounts)

F.No. IITR/F&A/355/21

Date: 21.07.2020

TO WHOM IT MAY CONCERN

Mridul's a prodigy! He has backed his book with strong research and this is one of the health book goals! This book makes you question yourself: Am I ready to change my life? Am I always fixated with the number of the weighing scale? and it will help you carve your own customised journey with just simple steps. I like its simple language and relatability! It's a gem for the shelf of health.

With best wishes.

21/7/2020

(G.K. Rastogi)
Joint Registrar
Finance & Accounts
IIT Roorkee

Dear Mridul,

I must congratulate you for writing such an informative and interesting book. It will be very useful during this COVID 19 when every one is talking about fitness & diet.

The way it's written goes straight to the heart of the reader

Keep exploring the world in your own way.

All the best.

Rohit Parasher

Ex SAI Football Coach

NS NIS PATIALA

भारतीय प्रौद्योगिकी संस्थान दिल्ली
INDIAN INSTITUTE OF TECHNOLOGY DELHI
हौज़ खास, नई दिल्ली-110016
Hauz Khas,New Delhi - 110016
Tel. : +91-11-26591758 (O)
E-mail : joint.registrar.ird.accounts@admin.iitd.ac.in

महेश कुमार गुलाटी
संयुक्त कुलसचिव (औ.अनु.वि.-लेखा)
M.K. GULATI
Joint Registrar (IRD - Accounts)

TO WHOM IT MAY CONCERN

This book transformed my perception on Health and I have also started looking at Food with the eye of reverence, rather Than thinking about it as just another Commodity in our lives· Indeed, it's a Knock on the door for our biased and Social-media shaped perceptions for food, Health and exercise· Thanks Mridul

Good Luck! It's a complete package for nor all Weight loss but overall health! Can't Believe this young child has covered up Each facet of transformation, including Exercise and sleep routines Children Including you are the future of our nation Keep going Well done!

We listen to everything these days· We Listen to music, People talking on social Media, others' conversations at parties and whatnot· But we never listen to our own body! Mridul's book on physical transformation has started well and he has included his realistic experiences on his weight loss journey I like how the content is organized· A book to keep for years as a handbook for health!

M·K GULATI

JOINT REGISTRAR

IIT DELHI

Dear Mridul,

Great to see your progress over the years from your thesis on fitness. Shall be grateful to get updated from your side. Keep it up. My good wishes and blessings !

Thanks & Regds,

MR. NARENDER KUMAR ALLANGH

DEPUTY MANAGER,

STATE BANK OF INDIA

CAG NEW DELHI

The Pill That Worked

MRIDUL SHARMA

Published By
Invincible Publishers

Published by
Invincible Publishers
201A, SAS Tower, Sector 38, Gurugram – 122003
Phone: +91-124-4034247, +91 9355675555
www.i-publish.in

This book is a work of non-fiction. Any resemblance to real persons, living or dead, or actual events or locations, is purely coincidental and the publisher does not hold responsibility for the same.

First edition – 2020

ISBN: 978-93-89600-94-0

Author's email: sharmamridul197@gmail.com

About the Author

Mridul Sharma is currently a Class 12th student at K.R. Mangalam World School, Vikas Puri, New Delhi; who is also a biology fanatic. He has attended Summer Programs at the University of Michigan Ann Arbor for the course "Catalysis, Solar Energy, and Green Chemical Synthesis" in 2018 and "Tissue Engineering" at Stanford University in 2019. He has also presented the paper titled "Effects of Exercise and Sleep on Learning" in a National Conference and presented and published the paper "Descriptive Study of the Role Played by Exercise and Diet on Brain Plasticity" in an International Conference held at Dubai, for which he received the Best Presenter award. In 6th grade, he was also telecasted on Zee News for the program "Meet Kids with Psychic Powers" for Extrasensory perception skills.

Content

Module 3: SLEEP PILL

Module 4: THE GRAND PILL

Module 5: Q & A SERIES

Acknowledgement

After losing weight and recovering back from the consequences of extreme calorie restrictions, I really wanted to put the science behind it, out to the world; so that we don't repeat history but grow together, hand in hand with our experiences. Without the support of my parents, my school, my teachers, and my friends, this wouldn't have been possible. Especially, my grany and my father.

Thanks to my parents and teachers for their guidance, my friends for enlightening me with some of the difficulties they had gone through while losing weight, and my school for the cooperation.

Preface

I was born and brought up in Delhi, and I HAVE been a foodie right from the beginning. 'Food guru', 'Foodie' were just a few of the many names I was addressed with. I always sought to bring a sense of novelty in my dishes, by sometimes adding diverse flavored sauces to it, and even combining different cuisines into one grand meal. I realise I had failed to look at the divine entity beyond the macroscopic level.

But looking back, it seems like it even wasn't the macroscopic appearance that actively appealed to my senses, which compelled me to produce diversity in my cuisines. It turns out that ever since childhood I had been a slave of my genes, repeating the drudged work over and over again: Eating. The appeal of the food isn't because we, as individuals consciously like it, but it is rather about what our genes like, and it has become our one primary mission: For Survival.

Now, since I wasn't conscious about what goes inside my body, it should also be a no brainer that my consciousness wasn't directed to what stays in the body: constituting my body weight. As a child, whenever I was asked to stand on the weighing scale, it wasn't me who wanted to know the statistics: It was always a second person thing; it was all about others and the image of myself. But, I actually never cared about the digits on the scale.

However, when I entered the 6th grade, I did develop a sense of concern over those landing numbers, I didn't become health conscious or anything, but because of social pressure. We started having annual medical checkups in our school, where they test our physical quantities, and (unfortunately, which later become fortunately) body weight was one of them. As I used to walk towards the medical room with my mates, I started having a panicky concern of how my weight would be perceived by my peers, and whatnot. As I would be asked to stand on the weighing scale, my mind wouldn't be having some new scientific thoughts or ideas running: since all the attention was directed to the numbers I would hear from the nurse's assistant who scrutinized the scale.

However, I made sure that I have to face such situations as less frequently as possible, so the only time I would stand on the weighing scale would be just once a year, and I would be so confident that I must have gained more weight that I would always be interested in knowing the rate of change more than the actual number.

Apart from the challenges at school, there were some other situations which put me into the self analyzing mode, at least temporarily. For instance, once upon a time, as I walked into the park to look for my friends, a couple of children approached me to take their ball beside me. The younger one proclaimed "Uncle's also here with us to play." As soon as I heard those words, my face turned pale and had a little laughter of worry. The elder one corrected him, and I thanked him and I cleared the spot in ignominy. I "fathomed" the issue and did what every normal person would do: "Hey Siri, set a reminder to run tomorrow at 7." But after seeing no displacement of the weighing scale, my willpower exhausted and I stopped.

Don't get me wrong. This wasn't the only attempt I made. I remember a couple of other times installing apps to record my cycling distance; cycled for a couple of days, and after seeing my efforts turning futile again, I'd point finger at my luck for not having a high enough metabolism and just move on.

From that moment until I lost, I was set in an idiosyncratic theory that whoever was "fit" must have a high metabolism. However, little did I know that things were about to take a U-turn in my 10th grade.

I applied to an exchange program in the middle of the 10th grade-KLYES-which would provide me the opportunity of studying for almost a year in the U.S at no cost, plus it'd be providing me the monthly stipends. It had a number of different rounds, each one growing more intricate on succession. I applied, cleared numerous rounds but couldn't get past through the second last round by a minuscule margin. Even though I was in utter despair, I decided to move on, until I got to know the precise reason why I couldn't qualify: Physical Fitness.

I vividly remember my trail of thought that day: as soon as I heard it, I was in utter disbelief, how can this even be significant criteria! They asked us for our essays, the extra-curricular, recommendations, and letters to host families, our home routines, conducted interviews, group discussions, and whatnot. But I gradually realized that the cursed pounds around my body were paradoxically going against my needs, the comments I had received regarding my weight were projecting in my mind in the precise sequence and my response to it.

Usually people set fitness goals whenever there's a new start-a festival, the New Year; however, I couldn't bear with those cursed pounds anymore. I have to get rid of it. My past frivolous efforts evolved into set, determined goals, and I did succeed. The journey was fun but it involved numerous causalities, including severe sickness.

After losing weight, I could feel myself as a different person. Not only did I feel lighter and more robust, I had the leverage to divert my psychic energy to some new task. However, my mind was still revolving around this weight loss. It wanted to know the reason beyond successful weight loss peculiar to this time only. It wanted the exact mechanisms behind weight loss, its role in our various hemispheres of our lives, and wanted to explore the deeper science behind it. As I started to invest my psychic energy in numerous online courses, research papers, my mind was exhilarated with how crucial it is and the countless connections just a mere weight loss can produce in our lives: enhancing learning, cognition (including preventing its decline), executive and decision making skills, protection from Alzheimer's, Parkinson's, eradicating depression, increasing mindfulness, and much remains unexplored as well!

While reading, writing research papers about the plethora of benefits we can experience through this one SINGLE objective, I realized the factors which cause weight loss (includes control over directive factors like exercise, diet, and indirect factors like sleep, mindfulness) are keystone habits, the habits which can impact other numerous habits. I realized not only the peers around me could deeply enjoy learning of their will, but they would also free their psychic energy on what they've previously been directing at stress and anxiety related issues.

I wanted it to spread this to my community and the world as fast as possible. So, after looking through some possible means, I decided this book will resonate with my intentions and be the source of conductance. I decided to include my personal experience and some science involved in weight loss, because studies have shown that people have a much better control over a thing if they know how it works, and I can testify to these studies as my weight hasn't fluctuated since the day I reached the golden number. My story will serve as a human voice behind that science, which will induce creativity and a sense of connectedness that if I can do it without a naturally high metabolism and spending even a penny, then any Homo sapien can.

FIT INDIA MOVEMENT:

Fit India movement is a nation-wide movement started by our Honourable Prime Minister Narendra Modi that focuses on motivating people to care about their personal well being. This movement is something that was so much needed in the current world, owing to birth of technology that was initially meant to improve our lives. While technology can't be separated, this movement could be something which could contribute in establishing the disturbed equilibrium yet again, and hence enable us to benefit from both sides of the era.

Even though my experiences served as the starting motor for the book, the Fit India movement acted as a catalyst in the process, helping me to bring it to the end.

And through this book, I wish to contribute more towards this movement and bring the next wave of fitness.

Module 1

DIET PILL

Chapter: 1

Introduction

"You didn't see that coming?" Of course, you could; I can't use the Avengers meme here because whenever we hear about health, the first things that come to our mind are exercise and diet. I will be talking about exercise a bit down the road, but right now, our discussion will revolve around "THE DIET". Now, what's the first thing that comes to your mind when you hear the word "diet"? The first thing I believe that comes to our mind before anything else is the classification of whether the diet is "healthy" or "not healthy". To test this on someone else, I asked my mother the same question "What comes first to your mind when you hear the word diet?" This 12-word long input gave me just a 2-word output: "nutritious diet". And I believe this should be the case for the most if not all. And actually, this sounds very logical, since we raise up the word diet only if we are either affected with some dietary issues, or we just are becoming too curious to know about it (or even both, like me ;)). And this is exactly what people started thinking about back in the 1900s too. Don't just fret yet, I will take you back in those days soon (just like the time machine in the endgame), but before going into the past, allow me to make you aware of the present (since this is what we care about the most, no?).

For starters, here are some relevant statistics: according to the WHO, 15 million people suffer from stroke every year, and out of that, 5 million die and 5 million are permanently disabled. One of the main identified reasons for stroke is high blood pressure, and its prevalence is reducing in developed countries. And bringing the diet into picture now, there are 1.7 million worldwide deaths just because of not having enough fruit and vegetable consumption as per WHO standards.

In terms of financial stock, we all are aware of the standards followed by the international agencies that categorize countries as developed or underdeveloped countries. But can the "development" factor also show some trends in the diet and food consumption of its citizens? Let's explore:

GLOBAL AND REGIONAL PER CAPITA FOOD CONSUMPTION (KCAL PER CAPITA PER DAY)

SER NO.	REGION	1964-1966	1974-1976	1984-1986	1997-1999	2015	2030
1	World	2358	2435	2655	2803	2940	3050
2	Developing countries	2054	2152	2450	2681	2850	2980
3	Near East and North Africa	2290	2591	2953	3006	3090	3170
4	Sub-Saharan Africa	2058	2079	2057	2195	2360	2540
5	Latin America and the Caribbean	2393	2546	2689	2824	2980	3140
6	East Asia	1957	2105	2559	2921	3060	3190
7	South Asia	2017	1986	2205	2403	2700	2900
8	Industrialized countries	2947	3065	3206	3380	3440	3500
9	Transition countries	3222	3385	3379	2906	3060	3180

(Transition countries includes South Africa)

It's clearly noticeable from the table above that the "industrialized" countries tend to be the greatest of calories consumers. But, down here is another chart which tells the percentage of prevalence of obesity in various parts of the world. It can be seen that a higher number of intake of calories clearly corresponds to the prevalence of obesity like it is shown in developed countries like the U.S and Northern African region.

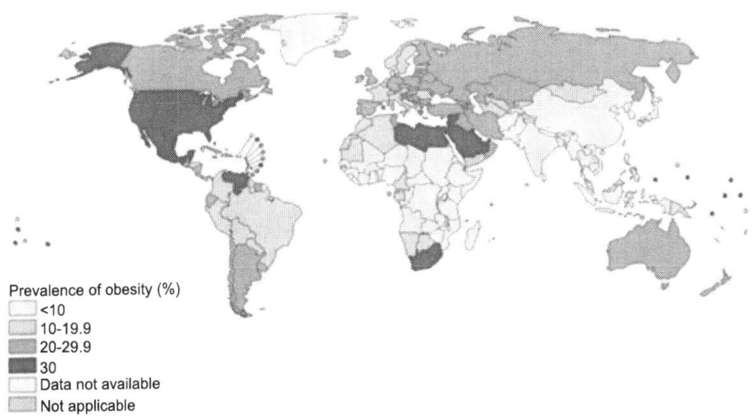

After being thorough with the facts, it's time to understand why actually food is so important to us.

We all must have heard that saying consisting of 3s: "You can live only 3 minutes without air, 3 days without water, and 3 weeks without food." So there must be something special in the food on which our whole life is staked on (Of course, the other two are also super important, it's just that I don't want to divert off the topic, by going out of this book's spectrum ;)). In 1827, British physician William Prout ended up adding other 3 to this chain: the food consists of 3 macronutrients for survival. They are proteins, carbohydrates, and fats. But ever since that, it seems like most of us are more concerned with these 3 macros majorly, rather than the food as a complete whole, which has led to the invention of supplements concentrated with one kind of nutrient rather than the whole. And the reason why this is disturbing will be discussed later in this chapter too. But for now, let's first understand what these 3 macros are in the first place.

One of the biggest and the foremost mistakes people make is by assuming that these macros stay forever in their definite shapes and therefore, can't ever be converted into the other. We forget to consider the fact that everything that goes into our body is broken down into finer substances in order to release energy.

And don't worry, I thought it this way too that too much protein would prevent me from getting fat as it would be "only" used in building my body and would not add up to fats. So, during my weight loss period, taking protein powder was also one of my decisions. Another example could be regarding fats, which usually get stored, can also be broken down and converted into a substrate in the glucose breakdown pathway to release energy (if this sounds a bit tedious, don't worry. Knowing the fact that they are interchangeable will do too). Anyway, it's now the time to look at each macro individually (to establish the base, I will discuss a little bit of biology for each of the 3 macros, no need to freak out if you aren't biology-friendly!):

Carbohydrates: These are basically long chains of saccharides called polysaccharides. As we intake the food, these polysaccharides are broken down into glucose which contains 2 saccharides in it. This process is necessary because the breaking of substances leads to production of energy in our bodies (don't break anything in your home in an inspiration, after reading this).

Proteins: As we learned Carbs are made of long chains of saccharides, similarly Proteins are made of long chains of amino acids. These amino acids can also be broken down and be used to build lean tissues, do the repair work, and some other functions. But don't forget that its excess intake can be converted into fat stores in our body (excess of everything is bad :)).

Fats: Like the above two, fats consist of long chains of a combination of glycerol and 3 fatty acids. These can also be broken down to release energy. Now if you're paying attention, there's one problem: if all of the 3 substances have the capability to break down to release energy, why is it just the fats, which form chunks around our body parts? The reason is that out of the 3 macros, fats have the most energy-dense storage mode. This can be proved by the fact that for every gram burnt, fats provide 9 calories, whereas carbs and proteins provide only 4 for every gram. This has led our body to evolve in a way to prefer to store more and more fats, which has led to obesity.

By now, I hope you must have established a sense of what diet is, and its components in classified form. But as I said earlier, focusing on the food as a whole will be a lot beneficial in the long run than considering them consisting of just some individual parts. So, soon we would be bringing these 3 macros back into play, but this time as a part of food as a whole (hence, less biology there!). This would help you think about why I am stressing more on the food in general.

Chapter: 2

Debunking the Truth

After World War 2, many socio-cultural changes took place in the society and the food industry too couldn't stay immune to these for long. With the increase in demand of food production, these industries started producing inexpensive food in bulk quantities. And at the same time, women, who earlier were managing the family food preparation, started stepping out of their homes and their numbers significantly increased in the workforce. This led to a decline in cooking at home, and since those "inexpensive/ ready to cook" foods were loaded with calories, the daily total calorie intake also increased. These dramatic changes in our diet led to a rapid emergence of obesity in society, and as a result, increased medical recommendations addressing this epidemic also.

The journey of these recommendations started in the U.S. by Dr. Ancel Keys, who, on his journey around the globe, noticed the varying rates of heart diseases with varying countries. This kindled curiosity of his gave birth to one of the earliest researches in this line, which was called the "Seven countries study" (and in fact, it's still in continuation even today since 1958!). The seven countries studied included 4 different parts of the world: US, Northern Europe, southern Europe, and Japan, and included a total of 12,736 males in 16 cohorts, aged between 40 & 59. One of the earliest findings of this study highlighted a very low rate of heart diseases in Crete (a Greek island) and high rates of those in the U.S. and Eastern Finland. So, Dr. Keys plotted the graph depicting the link between fat consumption and heart disease and found that lower the fat consumption, the lesser was the heart disease rate (lowest being in Japan for the lowest fat consumption).

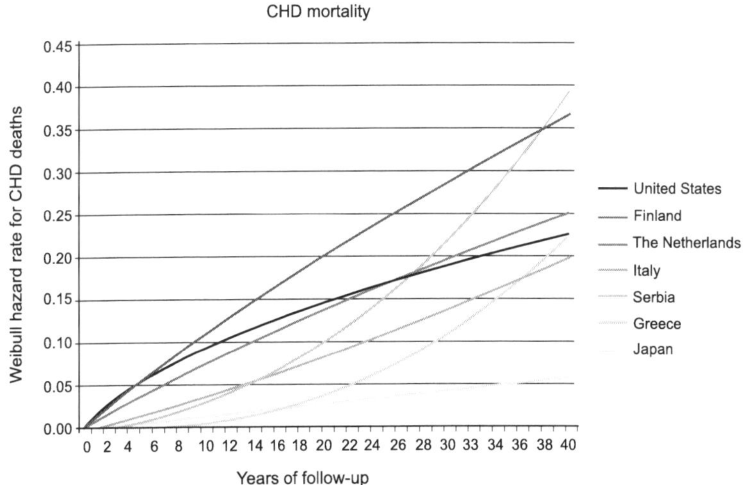

CHD (Coronary heart disease) is a certain type of heart disease (Appendix).

This breakthrough activated various drastic changes that were being implemented by the governors in the U.S., resulting in designing of the first Food Guide Pyramid that guided the public to cut down the fat consumption and replace it with the grains in the form of wheat, bread, pasta in 7-11 servings per day (later, these were also adopted by the WHO). Due to less public awareness, people started sticking with the guidelines and ate more and morecarbs, and increased their sugar intake from sugarcane.

In order to simulate the experiment and relate it to the mortality, Dr. Key designed another experiment called "Minnesota Coronary Experiment" involving 6 Minnesota state hospitals, 1 nursing home with 4393 men and 4664 women, all institutionalized. He divided the participants into 2 groups: one receiving low and the other high saturated diet. To make this experiment more realistic, both the groups received food that had same extrinsic features so that even the doctors and the staff didn't know the difference. After continuing this trend for 4.5 years, the experiment looked for various cues in the group: hardening of arteries in the vascular region which leads to arteriosus chlorotic heart disease, strokes in the central nervous system, cardiac arrest-related deaths, and cues for hypertension on the heart, kidney, clots in the heart and more. The results produced were astonishing: There was no difference in the rate of disease amongst both the groups (and in some cases, the diet-restricted group did worse than the non-restricted), especially in women!

Another study that was going on around the same time included 458 patients suffering from Coronary heart disease. They also divided the participants into 2 groups: one which received 9.8% of the total calories from saturated and 15% from polyunsaturated fats, and 13.5% and 8.9% respectively for the other. Upon completion of the study after 5 years, most of subjects lost weight, changed their dietary plans, and even quit smoking. The results unveiled astonishing results yet amplified the confusion produced by Dr.Keys's study: the overall survival rate was better in the group which consumed saturated fats!

Now at this point, people became more dumbstruck than ever: what they thought as the culprit for long is not what they should have been avoiding in the diets! To put the pieces of the puzzle together, various statisticians who took part in the seven countries study, reconsidered the patterns of mortality now in 22 countries, but still found that the lowest mortality nation was Japan which indeed was the nation who consumed the lowest fats!

But the paradoxical game wasn't just over yet. Researchers started reviewing previously collected data to check for any other clues that they might have missed. Ramsden, a researcher at the University of Alabama reviewed the data of Minnesota Coronary experiment and went over hundreds of data. He concluded that higher the cholesterol in a diet, higher is the autopsies rate, and less consumption of saturated fats corresponded to more deaths. Not only this, Ramsden reviewed the data of other studies as well like the Sydney Heart Study of Australia, and found some similar results of inverse relation between fats and the mortality rate. He went on further and reviewed almost all the dietary intervention studies which tended to replace saturated fats with unsaturated fats; like LA Veterans Study, The Rose Corn Oil Trial, the Medical Research Council Soy Study, etc. And after all this work, he found consistent results: there was either no effect on the cholesterol levels by the intervention of unsaturated fats or it was better off to be on control.

Another researcher who was part of the Seven Countries study, studied the number of people affected or died by strokes after 20 years of the experiment, and found only the age and blood pressure to be the determinant, NOT the cholesterol levels.

At this stage, if you were not having a dynamic day where you'd switch places form one corner to another, I bet this drama must have been enough to drive you to delirium!

With the passage of time, more the scholars were trying hard to get closer to the truth, the more it seemed like they were getting entangled in it. Checked for the relation of fats with strokes-no results, checked relation between types of fats-no results, checked if the source of fat produced any mutation to their continuing streak, but-no results, and finally also checked if the quantities of consumption(one or more than once a week) could be the magic key, but...

Some of the scholars began to realize that it was time to look at the foods as a whole and not as a collection of some individual components like fats; to see if that produced any variation in the patterns of mortality and strokes.So, a national population-based longitudinal study by the University of Alabama was conducted which kept track of about 30,000 African American and Caucasian adult population (they chose this group because studies have shown that African Americans had disproportionately high stroke cases). This time, they compared the effects of food groups on strokes and mortality and categorized food into the following groups: fast food, southern, plant-based, alcohol, and sweets. This led them to the results that the southern diet consumers were the most susceptible to mortality and strokes while the plant-based diet consumers were on the least side. This startled them to even compare the diet relative to numerous other factors including age, race, sex, education, income, smoking, and lifestyle. And all these produced coherent results to the former one. Hence, this led the American Medical Association to edify their past recommendation of consuming low-fat diet (although they still kept consumption of saturated fat recommendation to less than 10%).

So long story in short: It's actually not the fats which are the actual CULPRIT in this scenario. Proteins, one of the other macros isn't the culprit either, since these are what we are made up of and these have remained the same. So, only one remains… THE carbohydrates!

The Carbs or the Devils?

Recall that after the food pyramid recommendations, people increased their carbs intake, which came majorly from cereals, and even much higher consumption of high fructose corn syrups. And not just the people, but even the food industries started cutting down the fats from their foods and started adding higher amounts of corn syrup to it (to still make it taste good :/). Hence the reason behind the exponential increase in obesity became evident: it is the sugar which increases obesity, diabetes, and inflammation response in our brain. But how does that happen actually?

Chapter: 3

Body's Reaction to Food

Let's come out of the previous story and see what happens inside our body as we eat food. We all know that the macros don't really stay in their 'pre-defined' state. Carbs breakdown and are converted directly, all into the glucose, but only some of the proteins and fats are converted into glucose. There's a major hormone secreted in our body secreted by the liver which plays a major role in the balancing of the glucose levels in our blood: insulin (theirs is another hormone involved in blood glucose homeostasis but let's keep that out of discussion as of now). But why should we even care about blood glucose levels in the first place? Well, higher blood glucose levels lead to hyperglycemia which basically is the defining characteristic of the DIABETES (So, this definitely establishes some respect for the hormone which is doing all the big god work in our body!). Most of the glucose in our blood is taken up by the muscle cells since they need more energy to perform work, and this topic is also discussed further in the exercise chapter.

Insulin is the key that basically promotes cells to intake the glucose by binding to its receptors present on the cell surface which is nothing more than like the key-lock system (insulin as key and the receptor being the lock). If insulin is doing its job correctly, how does it even matter how high our blood glucose levels are, until there's no defect in the insulin lock itself!

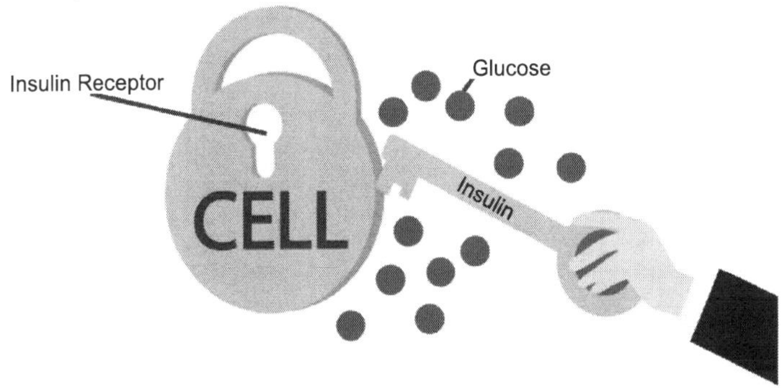

The above image is a simplified description of the intricate process that insulin participates in. Insulin opens the cell's gates, thereby allowing influx of glucose thus normalizing the blood glucose levels.

It turns out, accumulation of blood glucose is not necessarily induced by a defect in the insulin receptor, i.e. the accumulation can happen even when the insulin is working just fine. Here's how the things work: as insulin binds to its receptor, it opens a channel for the blood glucose to pass in. This channel works on the concentration gradient, i.e. it allows the flow of glucose only because the outside concentration is high, and substances tend to move towards lower concentration. Now there will be a point when the concentration is balanced, hence this stops the flow of glucose inside the cells and hence leads to its accumulation in the blood. This building up of glucose in the blood is sensed by the liver and hence it secretes more insulin to let open more and more channels for that abandoned glucose. Once this is not effective as well, the body then tries storing the glucose in the form of glycogen stores in the liver (which can be used later, when needed) and also converts the carbs to the fats, by a process called de novo lipogenesis.

Once these fat cells become too big, they start getting deposited by the organs and this process starts with the liver, leading to a serious condition called Fatty Liver. And this is no joke because leaving it untreated can lead to liver failure! But those big stacks of masses aren't just sufficed there. After the liver, they also start building up in the blood vessels and hence disturbing the balance in their relaxation and contraction (the importance of contraction and relaxation of blood vessels is discussed in the exercise chapter). And as you can imagine someone calling for help when in trouble, these vessels also call 911 (yes, not 100 since they need an immediate response! :p) thereby activating our immune system cells to treat it, which is called as an inflammatory response.

The first time I read all about this, the only thing I was wondering was that how could all this mess be avoided? All of these things happening in the body, those triggered responses, fatty liver, etc. were all because of the development of one thing: insulin resistance.The name describes it well; this is a condition that leads to a lesser intake of glucose even in the presence of higher amounts of insulin.This is a condition which appears years before you see diabetes.

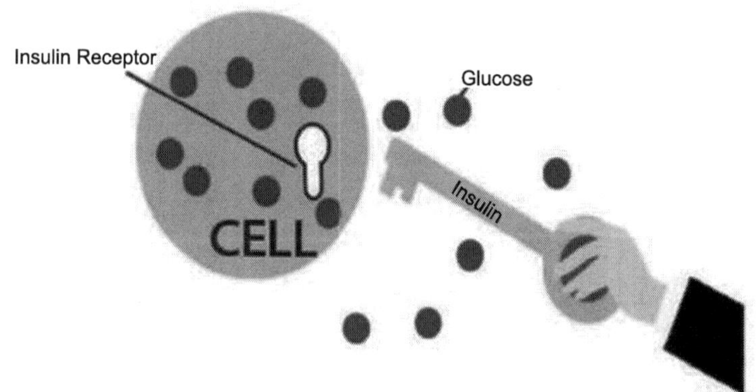

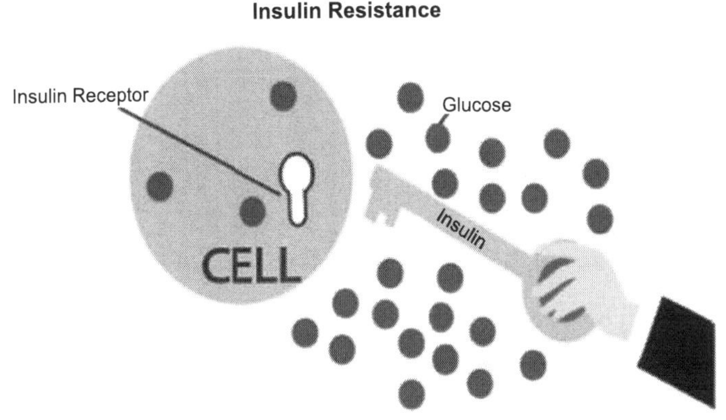

This image perfectly describes the insulin resistant condition. When there's normal insulin metabolism, the gates open and close perfectly.However, the gates malfunction in the insulin resistant state causing piling of insulin in the blood.

Scientists back in the time began exploring other functions of insulin, in order to see to what extent the damage of insulin resistance can be extended to. They found that besides promoting the formation of glycogen stores in the liver when there is abundant glucose, it also controls a process called lipolysis. This stops the conversion of fats to fatty acids for energy production and starts relying on the presently available glucose.

Exploring insulin's role in organ systems, scientists thought that the brain is the only organ in our body that could not be affected by insulin resistance. But the latest results have shown some contrasting results: insulin is not only used for metabolism in the brain, but also mediates the neural growth cascades. That means it promotes neurogenesis (formation of neurons) and inhibits its apoptosis (prevents degeneration).

As we have now explored a significant influencer inside us, the insulin, it surely makes a difference when we know what we eat and what happens in the body subsequently. This mental model should tug you subconsciously when you next grab that cheese sandwich loaded with carbs!

Chapter: 4

Basal Pillars of Diet

As I had said in the introduction, focusing on food as a whole should be our main goal. And I believe the medical industry all around the world can show drastic improvements if doctors just modify a couple of key terms in their suggestions, i.e. by replacing the usage of the individual nutrient supplements, and really talk about food. With that in mind, let's spill some more beans on macros now, as the constitutional parts of the diet.

Carbohydrates: As we had read about the research done in the past, we came to the conclusion that it was the Carbs actually who were the main culprits,including added sugars in our drinks, food, bread, and the list keeps going. But there's one group of food which although is rich in Carbs but, according to research, carries miraculous effects: the fresh juicy fruits straight from the farm. There are other food types as well which are rich in these culprit macros but still seem to have been proven beneficial for us: the whole grains like brown rice and rolled oats. So, what's peculiar about these food groups which though consist of proven felons, and yet manage to generate a transformation in us?

The speciality is that these foods, along with the Carbs, are also rich in fiber which retards the rate of glucose releasing into the bloodstream, hence a suppressed insulin response. And this leads me to introducing another term called glycemic index. Glycemic index of a food is basically the rate at which it releases the glucose into the blood. Foods generally have a lower glycemic index when they are rich in fibers or are taken with fats and proteins.

While on the other hand, foods rich in refined carbs including soda, bread, etc. have a higher glycemic index which inflates the insulin levels leading to insulin resistance.

Fats: The dietary fats can also be divided into 2 categories: saturated and unsaturated fats, and I think you must have seen me mentioning it a couple of times before too. So, by their differing names, where do you think lies the key difference between both the types: is it the density, or something mixed in it in varying proportions or what? The answer is, indeed, the density: in the cases of saturated fats, they are solids at room temperature like butter, etc. whereas the unsaturated fats are liquids like oil, etc. If you remember the fact that the macro intake doesn't necessarily stay in their "pre-defined macro state" in our bodies, it is safe to say that even if we don't eat fats, our body can induce other macros to turn into fats and meet its requirements. But there's one glitch, there's this one kind of fat that our body can't synthesize, hence leaving only one way to get the benefit of those fats: by externally consuming them. These special fats are called omega-3 fatty acids. They are found in fishes, flax seeds, nuts, etc.

As we advanced in the technology, people figured out innovative ways to artificially make unsaturated fats. But why unsaturated fats and not saturated fats? Since we know saturated fats are solids at normal temperature, they are more likely to cause blockage in our body than the unsaturated fats. But the problem with the induced unsaturated fats is that the chemical bonds we artificially make are less stable and switch themselves into trans rather than cis- orientation (if you're wondering what all this is, don't! Just some scientific jargon!)

Hence, they have the name- Transfat.

The thing to know about Trans fats is that they are the last thing you want to have. They not only increase the LDL (Low Density cholesterol/ bad cholesterol) cholesterol levels but also decrease the HDL (high density cholesterol/ good cholesterol) cholesterols leading to the formation of plaques in the arteries. The thing which makes trans fats even more perilous than the saturated fat is that though the saturated fat also promote LDL formation, it does not decrease the HDL levels. Hence, it becomes imperative on our side to stay away from Transfat as much as possible.

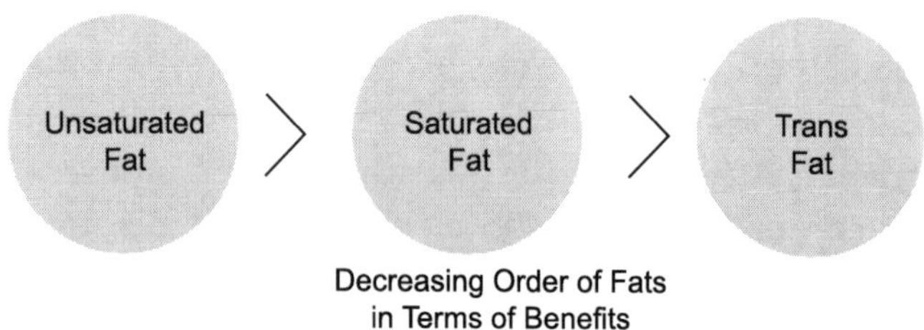

Decreasing Order of Fats in Terms of Benefits

Proteins: We are familiar with the basic constituent of protein, the amino acids. But amino acids can be classified in 2 categories: essential, and non-essential, depending on whether they can be synthesized by our body or not. Those amino acids that can be synthesized by our body are classified as non-essential amino acids, and those which need to be replenished by external sources are called essential amino acids. Now don't let the names befool you: when I say non-essential, it doesn't mean your body doesn't require them, it's just that your body is capable of meeting its own needs of those specific groups of amino acids. So, in order to fulfill the body's requirement of the amino acids that it can't synthesize, we need to eat proteins from animal and plant sources. Now there's further classification of proteins based on the source they are derived from: complete and incomplete proteins. The animal derived proteins are called complete, and the plant ones are called incomplete proteins. You might feel at this moment that

I am playing "the term game" with you, but believe me, I am not. And I will also say that don't let the "name" be the judgmental factor in someone's characteristics, this also applies to proteins too. The studies have shown that substituting plant based proteins in our diet for a few days a week significantly reduces the risk of falling short of essential amino acids.

Apart from that, vegetarian food sources are rich in fibers and low in saturated fats. But you might be like, "Hang on a sec, I think we just discussed that the fats were not the main culprit in the rise of obesity, so how does the quantities of saturated fat matter anyway?" If you look above, you see how Trans fats are more dangerous than the saturated fats for numerous reasons. But if you pay close attention, saturated fats also carry harmful properties like elevating LDL cholesterol levels. Other studies have also shown that people, who eat majority of the time plant based proteins, also have greater longevity than the animal protein eaters. And what's more: if the animal proteins are processed, it can actually cause damage like causing hardening of our arteries, increment in sodium levels contributing to high blood pressure, etc.

However keep note that relying too much on one thing doesn't produce the best results; do not be excessively picky! Go ahead and get those macros and relish nature's offsprings in their puerile form. The ideal protein diet should also include some animal sources like fishes, but the majority of the portion needs to come from the greens!

Chapter: 5

All That Glitters is Not Gold

I bet by this line, some of you might have started asking the question 'what makes processed food evil for us?' I mean if you really go by the name, something that is too much processed tends to be better as we get rid of non-substantial things, like impurities in the water. And actually that's what happens with the foods as well. Processing removes some components from the food, but those are basal components like the fibers, which we just talked about, with how they are important for preventing insulin resistance, and also removing other substances like iron, vitamin B, etc.

But what makes industrialists do something that is causing devastating effects on mankind? The answer is simple: Money. What else would you expect from industrialists anyway? By removing the substances mentioned above, it helps them in 2 ways: firstly, it gives foods a texture and hence, makes them look more appealing, and secondly, it increases the shelf life of the products, by decreasing their spoilage rates.

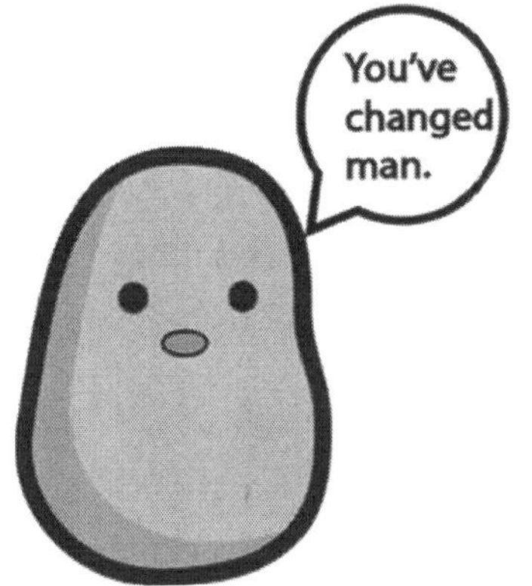

From our very early years, we have been always taught that humans are the most intelligent and capable animals on this planet. But I can show you one way in which even the insects like flies, bacteria, and fungi (which don't even have brains) are far more intelligent than us. Hard to believe, right? As I just mentioned above, processed foods have lower spoilage rates, i.e. the amount of nutrient content is directly related to the spoilage rate. But why? Well, when we see mold or some crazy stuff growing in the food, we call the food to be spoilt, and to slow that, we usually keep the foods in the refrigerator. This is done to slow down the rate of external agents feeding on the food hence preserving them. Now, if I keep an apple and a pizza slice together outside, which one would you see getting blackened out first? Of course, it would be the apple. This tells us that even the bacteria and other vectors around don't prefer to devour on something we've been eating mindlessly.

That was just one reason why I discussed that processed foods shouldn't be your first choice. Another way industrialists tend to maximize their profit margin is by using the cheapest raw materials possible. This can be proven by keeping a homemade pizza and an ordered pizza outside and checking for their spoilage rate. Over here as well, the market pizza is the one which lasts longer.

But of course, you might not always be leaving the food out and waiting for the bacteria to invade, and then decide if it's healthy or not…that's just too much of hassle! A more conceptual way for making healthy decisions is by looking at the food's nutrient density. This is nothing else, but the ratio of total nutrients in the food per total number of calories in the food. For example, carrots have high nutrition density since they provide more number of nutrients for every calorie intake.

BUT WAIT… WE ALL KNOW THAT IN SOME COUNTRIES LIKE THE U.S, A HEALTHY SALAD BOWL IS MUCH EXPENSIVE THAN A BURGER. WHY IS THAT SO?

When we say that salad is more expensive than a burger, we are basically talking in terms of cost per calories. But there's one thing we don't realize: those big buns are way more expensive if we look at cost per nutrient density. Because they are empty calories, their consumption actually is more as if on an epidemic.

If we look through this, we can clearly see that this is yet another tactic of those demon creators who are trying out every possible strategy to eat their bread and even own it!

Hence one takeaway from this part is to change the lens with which you had been looking towards diet for years, and appreciate the beauty of non polished natural foods.

LESS OF THIS

MORE OF THIS

Chapter: 6

Mission Impossible

After spotting the disguised species that make us hollow from the inside, it comes without saying that cutting down the sugar intake is our primary goal, isn't it? But how? How do we expect ourselves to cut down the sugar intake without even knowing the major source it's coming from? This sounds like an absurd question since who on Earth would not know that the sugars are mainly in the desserts and those sweets, chocolates, right? Err....Give me one sec. I am not saying this is erroneous. The graph does show that 20% of the sources of sugar are those lollies you'd been eating since childhood. But what about the other 80? Seems like those "side drinks" we have with our food also have a very significant contribution. But how did processed foods carry half of the total sugar even if they don't taste sweet? Foods like bread, chips, salad dressings, sauces etc., all contain significant amount of sugars.

So, **how much of the sugar are we recommended to have**? According to the WHO, everyone should consume sugar less than 10% of their total caloric intake. You can even cut it down to 5% of the total calories for bonus points. This sugar intake includes sugars from all the sources mentioned on the pie graph above like those syrups, drinks, etc. But as usual, there's one exception to this recommendation: there's no limit on the consumption of intrinsic sugars. Now, before you head out to buy all those sugar stocks, hear me out. Most, if not all, of us have been eating this since pretty much the entire time and most of us have it stocked in the houses all the time. If you still weren't able to guess it, the simple answer lies in the simplicity only: the fruits. Those fruits, which are available to us, turns out, do not harm us at all irrespective of the quantity intake, and this is what the science says.

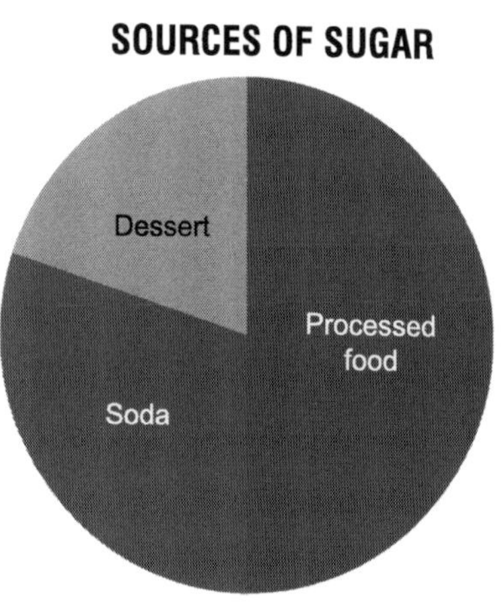

But it is also important to know how much of the artificial sugar we can have as intake and still be fine. So for an average person consuming 2000 calories a day,5% of it would be 100 calories from the sugar. Every gram of sugar gives around 4 calories, hence yielding you about 25 grams per day. In order to convert grams into teaspoons, just divide the number by 4, giving you 6 teaspoons a day. This number might make you feel like "Ah, I am safe, no worries!", but hang on there! As I said mentioned above, we don't even realize how much hidden sugar we are eating every day, even in the items which DO NOT taste sweet. For example, consider the image of this tasty berry flavored yoghurt below (don't ask me what brand it is of, I just googled it up) :

Looks mouthwatering, right? And also the size of the container doesn't seem to hurt at all; it's just one small cup. But, if you look closely on the nutritional label on the side, the sugar content in this one serving is 27g making about 108% of your total intake! It's that easy to get those seemingly sweet demons.

Talking of labels leads to yet another technique that those shrewd industrialists employ to fool you. By the law, companies are now required to disclose all the sugar quantities they used on a nutritional label, like shown above. But, they have figured yet another way out to basically "hide" the total sugar content from the consumers by not violating the law. That is done by using various forms of sugar and hence allowing them to break the big number into parts. For example, malt syrup, sucrose, maltose, lactose, corn syrup, dextrose, fructose, fruit juice concentrates, etc. are all other names of the DEATH (though some of them I just mentioned can be useful which I have talked about in the cheat sheet).

So, let me summarize and include some more sources from which you should take the sugar and which you shouldn't:

AVOID:

1. All the processed foods, desserts, and soda drinks.
2. The juice extracted from fruits (like oranges, etc.) even at home. This is because when we extract the juice, we basically throw away the pulp which is the main source of fiber. Throwing away fiber actually makes them no better than those packed brands.
3. Desserts including ice creams and all those sweets out there (including Indian).
4. All the carbonated drinks available out there- AS MUCH AS POSSIBLE.

HIGH FRUCTOSE CORN SYRUP= EVIL

Before you go ahead and buy foods composed of the substances mentioned in the cheat sheet, I want to remind you again that artificial form of any of those is equal to DEATH!

1. **Fructose**: This form of sugar is in the…yep fruits! Some of its NATURAL sources are sugar cane, honey, apples, etc. and in the vegetables like onions, chicory roots. The high fructose sources foods include apples, grapes, watermelon, asparagus, peas and zucchini. And, if you're fructose intolerant, you can have an intake of low fructose foods like bananas, blueberries, strawberries, carrots, avocados, green beans and lettuce.

But when should we not consume fructose rich foods, or let me restate the question: what are the foods that contain fructose which we must avoid at any cost? But before we dig in into the soil to explore the food types, it's time for some science to apply behind what the high fructose diet leads to. Unlike glucose which is triggered by our body when we intake and release insulin to break it down, it turns out there's no "insulin" in our body for fructose. To add a cherry on top, this monosaccharide also does not trigger the feeling of fullness in our body (this law doesn't apply to fruits, so bring in some more colors!). Now if your biology usually supports you, you might ask that there needs to be some place in our body where fructose can be broken! There is, which is the one and only liver. The high fructose quantities when hit the liver all in one go, it becomes intuitive that this is not what your body wants. And if I were to answer you for the question of why the fruits are exception to the rule, I have 2 reasons on the table:

I. First thing is that they don't have massive high levels like the foods I am going to discuss in the exceptions to the cheat sheet, plus they easily make us satisfied.

II. Second thing is since they have high fiber content in them, they slow down the rate of exposure of fructose to the liver and hence make things cooler!

EXCEPTIONS WITH SOME OF ITS OWN NESTED EXCEPTIONS:

Let me take you back in the time (ah, I am a good time traveler!) to see how the fructose rich foods came into existence. So, it all started with that farmers started to grow more and more corn (because of some political reasons which I am avoiding to put here) and then they reached a point when they had crazy amounts of corn of no use. And this is where (un)luckily, the scientists stepped in to make "good" use of it. They processed and refined it, and came up with a sugar alternative called High Fructose Corn syrup (HFC are composed of equivalent quantities of fructose and glucose, you get the sense by now that the names can be misleading). Since this was considered as a "sugar alternative" becausc of its same caloric value and structure at molecular level, they actually started replacing this with the table sugar since HFCs were cheaper in production. But researchers at Princeton University did studies on rats,comparing the effects of HFC and the regular sugar. The study found out that HFC fed rats had higher fat deposition in their body leading to weight gain. Now for those of you who are really into the fiction, you might imagine the scientists who created this as being wicked and having a disproportionate smile on their faces with horror background music. So, our biggest question of all time: how to stay safe from this invention?

Listed below is the list of items which have HFCs fused in them in some form or the other:

A. **Sodas**- By now, this comes without surprise. In a 350 ml drink, it has 13 sugar tea spoons (more than the double of the daily recommendation).

B. **Candies**- They are mostly sugar. Some companies add that in the form of HFCs (and the reason is quite intuitive).

C. **Salad Dressings**- Beware of these! From putting the first name as "Salad" to putting labels of low fat or fat free, the company makers of these products are constantly trying to make you fall in their trap. No doubt, they do shred the fat out of those, but to compensate, they add something deadly as you may have guessed: the HFCs.

D. **Frozen junk Foods-** Its name is already wicked enough.

E. **Bread**- This is something that we least expect to be sugary. But this also serves as an example of how something which doesn't even taste sweet may contain HFC and also emphasize the need to check for the food labels first (don't worry, I will explain how to do that as well).

F. **Canned FRUITS**- Although canned fruits also contain a lot of natural sugars in their fruits, unfortunately they also do have immense HFCs especially if they come soaked in syrups.

G. **Granola/Nutrition Bars**- Now suppose you are already tired playing sports all day long, and in the evening, when it's time to grind for the test the next day, you just don't feel like it. Now if you are someone who already knows that energy drinks must be avoided at all costs, you might want to turn to some other source which doesn't screw you up, plus gives you a boost to study. And what better could you think of if you have an energy bar sitting right around your desk's corner? You check the nutrition labels and it seems like what other place could be better than to find tons of nutrients in this 2X3X4 bar! The backside scene is that they all are just using oats mixed with additive sugar and supplemented nutrients which don't seem to do that much of a benefit. However, there are some brands out there which just use whole grain foods.

H. **Energy/Sport Drinks-** As explained with the above example, this also does more harm than good.

I. **Ice cream-** If you consume it in moderation, then you should be fine.

After going through this list, some of you might start

questioning then what else do we even have which does not contain HFCs apart from fruits? To recommend quick substitutes, you can have sparkling water instead of juices; replace your morning breakfast cereals with oatmeals, and use olive oil, balsamic vinegar and lemon juice as replacements for salad dressings. Personally, I eat most of the foods listed above. So does that mean I am breaking my own rules, or just messing around with you? No, the exceptional hack is to reduce both the frequency and the quantity of their intake. I honestly can't recall when was the last time I had my ice cream (of course, like a month or 2 before, not years!) and in terms of bread, I have it once in like 10 days. The rule I followed during the weight loss had somewhat this essence in common: if I had pizza that day, I would set a limit that I won't order it at least for 2 months. Simply, I just make my brain wired in a way that I just can't have it for another 2 months. Firmly talking to myself not only made me control the cravings (I usually don't do that now but before losing weight that was my life), but also helped me gain more control over myself. And if.... if somehow my puerile brain managed to break the law, I had the punishment written down, yes, actually written down which would be the same even if I had no other chance, on even a day before the 2 month mark. The punishment involved additional exercise or extension of deadlines of "polished" foods.

If you're wondering what if I just keep breaking rules like in a chain reaction, then I would be falling in the mode of collapse which would mean that losing weight is not a goal anymore. I have covered this chain reaction possibility in the Grand Pill.

THE CHEAT SHEET

Here, I have discussed the broad spectrum of items that can be relied upon.

Also, there are some surprise food ingredients that you may have least expected to be a part of this list (trust me, even I was baffled at first too). So, I decided to list it separately from others.

1. **Good' ol Glucose**: This is most favorable of all sugar forms which even our body can produce on its own with the help of interconversions of macros I talked about earlier. In order to create some reservoirs of food, it is the glucose which is stored in the complex forms. The glucose in the natural foods can be eaten without worrying about it. However, if you are already a diabetic patient, you might want to limit your fruit intake to 2-4 servings a day. And, some of the glucose rich sources include mangoes, bananas, etc.
2. **Lactose:** Lactose is nothing else but the sugars present in the milk. I didn't mention about the milk earlier that this is the drink which you can drink at pretty much anytime (don't forget that excess of everything is bad). Most of us have the enzymes to digest this lactose, so milk is not the problem. But…have you heard your friend say "I am Lactose Intolerant"? If yes, he's amongst those who shouldn't be taking lactose products since he doesn't have the required enzymes to digest it. In fact, every 3 out of the 4 people in this world are lactose intolerant with its prevalence higher in countries that don't have the European descent, like Asia.

But have you ever heard there are 2 types of dairy products: The Low fat and the full fat? Let me expand a bit on that, by explaining the advantages, and a couple of disadvantages as well of eating dairy products. The high fat dairy includes butter, whole milk and the low fat dairy includes skimmed milk, no-fat or low fat yoghurt, cottage cheese, etc.

First of all, humans are the only ones who consume milk even in adulthood! In fact, we started to consume dairy products as adults only after the agricultural revolution that allowed opened opportunities to raise more cows. And this is the reason why dairy is strictly excluded from the paleo diet (a form of diet). But as I mentioned above, most of the world can't consume dairy in the first place, so only a few people actually can take dairy. But what's in those items, which makes them included in highly recommended food?

Well, there's more than just lactose in those. For example, 235 ml milk is composed of 28% RDI (recommended daily intake) of calcium, 24% RDI of vitamin D, 26% RDI of Vitamin B12, and much more. What's more, cows that are fed with grass have more of the omega 3 fatty acids and 500% greater conjugated linoleic acid in their milk (remember that different dairy products can have much different composition)! As I mentioned before, omega 3-fatty acids are the only fats which our bodies don't synthesize and hence it's super important for us to look for the external agents. But what about conjugated linoleic acid? Does it also have a lengthy list of benefits like its name? I recommend you to explore by yourself :)

Before we get too distracted by these details, let me bring you back to the real deal: what about the dairy fat? As I had mentioned about 2 types of dairy fats,the full fat being the high in calories, whereas the low fat being low in calories; so which one out of the two do you expect to reduce the obesity and type 2 diabetes symptoms (aftermath of insulin resistance)? Before you flip this page away thinking I am asking you a super vague question, just WAIT……

Studies have shown that high dairy fat consumption is INVERSELY related to obesity! This claim is further strengthened by a study which showed that the participants who ate more full fat dairy products had lesser belly fat. And not only this, another study shows that this dairy increases insulin sensitivity resulting in a 62% lowered chance of type 2 diabetes.

EFFECTS ON HEART DISEASES:

As we looked at the effects of dietary saturated fats on diabetes, you must not be flabbergasted to know that these fats help in lowering the chances of cardiovascular diseases. But, things get mixed up a bit over here. Some studies also say that there's no existence of the link between these variables. However, a study in the U.S found out that these fats lead to increased risk of coronary heart disease. But, it may also be because of the fact that the effects of dairy on heart vary from country to country. This is because a study was conducted which found out that the countries in which cows are grass fed experience a significant cut down in heart diseases.But you might ask me: what's so special in those greens which we imagine crushing under our feet literally every single day? Well, the dairy products produced by cows which are fed grass in abundance, have vitamin K2 in them which is heart friendly. But still, at this moment we just can't be 100% sure that saturated fat dairies help in preventing heart diseases. The researchers have mixed opinions, whereas public health guidelines recommend us to minimize their consumption.

EFFECTS ON SKIN AND CANCER:

Okay, so I am hoping we all are aware of the fact that every fairy tale story has its own dark side, and nevertheless, this story of dairy fats also has its own. The consumption of dairy fat consumption leads to an increased acne on your skin. So for those of you who are over conscious about their skin, there you go. And talking about some big words like cancer, dairy products lead to an increment in the secretion of a protein called Insulin like Growth Factor-1 (IGF1). And studies have found that the increase of the IGF-1 levels lead to a higher risk of certain cancers. But wait, I know after reading this you may be much tempted to stop the dairy products all at once since that's the last thing you want to have. But, this is just half the information. The truth is that the relation between cancer and the dairy is intricate. For example, studies show that dairies reduce the risks of certain cancers like colorectal cancer but increase the risk of prostate cancer (don't worry, you don't need to know all those terms, though the google's right by the side:)). And, even this relation between prostate cancer and the dairy is uncertain. This is because some studies report that there is 37% increase in the prostate cancer risk while others say: Everything's chilling! And talking about the increased IGF-1 levels, they aren't all wicked either. These hormones are the ones you are looking for if you're trying to build up some muscle and strength. So the bottom line is, just don't stop consuming dairy, and if you're worried about acne, the treatment is just a click away.

If all this explanation didn't make much sense, let me summarize it in 2 lines: if you aren't lactose intolerant, then enjoy eating dairy, and prefer dairy from grass fed animals with no added sugar Period!

But what if you are lactose intolerant? You must be already thinking that you are just not entitled to have something of such benefit. But there's always a way out, and in this case it is the all time favorite, the Yoghurts!

YOGHURTS

Now this isn't a thing not to be known today, of course! But honestly, there are only a handful of peeps out there who can acknowledge how rich this is. Even I didn't know much about this rather than the fact that its current texture is a gift from bacteria called Lacto Bacillus, so if you're considering skimming over this section, I recommend you to hang on. By reading this, you might not only get a glimpse of its world's richness but also perhaps some of its downsides as well..... (Was that scary enough?)

To start, yoghurts basically come via the milk fermentation. It comes in a variety of types and some of those are found to be more beneficial than others.

1. Low fat or Non fat Yoghurts- The low fat yoghurts are made from 2% milk, whereas the non fat yoghurts are either made of no or skimmed milk. This is something lactose

intolerant people must consider.

2. Kefir- This is in the form of liquid yoghurt. This is probiotic yoghurt and can be easily prepared by adding kefir grains to the initial batch and leaving it for 12-24 hours. I have attached an image of a kefir grain for reference. Now just for the clarification purposes, some of you might start assuming that this is similar to Lassi. Though both are probiotic, Lassi only contains bacteria but the kefir contains bacteria as well as yeast.

   Bonus Tip: Although both Lassi and Kefir can be consumed interchangeably when in stable condition, if you are suffering from Diarrhea or you have loose stools, consuming Kefir might not be the best decision. Instead, Lassi will do the job better. Why? Because Kefir contains Yeast in it which tends to have a heating effect on our gastrointestinal tract (which can make hard stools softer).

3. Greek Yoghurt- This is the name not unheard of, thanks to 21st century marketing. This type of yoghurt is so wide spread, that some people might even have an assumption that it is the only yoghurt with no other types (yes I am a part of those "some people"). This yoghurt is creamy and is strained relatively higher than other yoghurts to decrease the water content in it. But there has to be something unique about this yoghurt for the industrialists to go crazy about this product. It is its high protein levels (since it's super dense, the protein level is almost double the level than that of the regular yoghurt) that they display in **bold** letters to increase their sales. Its advantages extend further as they

have less sugar levels (nearly half of the regular yoghurts) and this must be the first time those producers are making the right use of their publicity power. In addition to this, there is one more thing about this yoghurt which arguably adds another layer to its pile of benefits: its high relative fat content. Well thought overeating can be a problem, but high fat content ensures a higher satisfaction level and hence we are fulfilled in a less quantity (though, nowadays, greek yoghurt also has several varieties of its own including the variation in the fat levels).

But we all know nothing in the contemporary world is like 24 karat gold, so there has to be some cache over here as well, and there is indeed, one. As the greekyoghurts have relatively less water content, the removal of water does remove extra sugar but with it, this also reduces the nutrient levels of constituents like calcium. So if solely obtaining nutrients is your primary goal, you might want to try the regular version over greek.

4. Skyr- You may not have heard of this name before (neither did I before some time!). So, I am just writing it just for the sake of more options (since more, the better, with limits!).

   These are the Icelandic-style yogurt that are super dense and hence have high proteins. But these are made up by using 2-3 times higher milk quantity than the regular yoghurts, so this may not be the best choice for the Lactose intolerant people.

5. Frozen Yoghurts- This is a must-know type, not to be tried, but to be AVOIDED at all costs. Some people might call this as a "better" alternative to ice creams, but trust me, those are the things which only sound healthy. And if you think you are just the only one who thinks they are "better", you are not alone. A Survey in the U.S, which is one of the top 10 countries in terms of yoghurt consumption, found

out that 95% people think that frozen yoghurts are NICER than an ice cream! But the cold truth is that these fake substances can be actually more deteriorating for a number of reasons. Firstly, freezing yoghurts causes the natural live bacteria inside them to die and hence deprives us from the benefits of probiotics (though some of them do have added live bacteria but again, the proportion of probiotic frozen yoghurt is less). Secondly, have you observed that there's a debate going on whether frozen yoghurts should be preferred or not, over ice cream? So, if there's a debate, then the 2 products must share higher similarities than the differences. But can you ever imagine the natural yoghurt (if you haven't tasted it yet, then welcome to Earth) be palatable like ice cream? Of course, NOT! So, this tells us that these frozen yoghurts are also added with heavy loads of sugar just like the ice creams. And in fact, in order to compensate for their already not so sweet taste, frozen yoghurts on average have more sugar (17g per half cup) as opposed to those creameries (14g). And as a reminder, our daily consumption must fall under 25g of sugar.

6. Non Dairy yoghurts- Of course, if we have yoghurt that is especially not for lactose intolerants, there needs to be something exclusively for them, right? And yes, this yoghurt includes yoghurts made out of soy, coconut, etc.

But I know that all you care about are the benefits, so here they are:

1. Very rich in nutrients~ You name the nutrient, it has got it! But every best thing always lacks some or the other thing. In this case, it's the Vitamin D. Vitamin D is a crucial vitamin you get from the exposure to sunlight which helps in development of the immune system and increasing the bone strength.

2. Proteins are in there~ We all know the benefits of proteins, so I will better keep this part short. But, since the amount

of protein varies amongst different types of yoghurts, some yoghurts are naturally preferred over others.

3. Some types of yoghurts also contain good living bacteria, or probiotics, which really help the digestive system. These bacteria infected yoghurts (catchy name, right there) not only help in just general improvement but also help in fighting diseases and disorders. For example, yoghurts containing Lactobacillus and Bifidobacteria are known to lessen the effects of a disorder called Irritable Bowel Syndrome which causes abdominal pain and constipations.
4. Better immune system~ As said above, some types of yoghurts really provide much more benefits than others. In this case, the probiotic-rich yoghurts and the Vitamin D yoghurts are a boon for the immune system.
5. Helps in stronger bones (what else can I say about that?).
6. Weight management~ Since the yogurts are high in proteins, studies have found that protein, along with calcium, helps in stimulating hormones which suppress the appetite intake and hence fewer calorie intake automatically means weight loss. Apart from this, studies concerned with finding the patterns in the behavior of those who eat yoghurt are usually healthy eaters than non-yogurt eaters.
7. Lactose Intolerant~ Never mind, yoghurt has got your back. But, this applies to only some extent and only to some particular yoghurt types, mostly the probiotic ones which assist in digestion.

But apart from the starry and dramatic benefits, there seems to be some dark sides linked to yogurts as well.

1. The most common no-no for yoghurts is the added sugar. Naturally, yoghurts are loaded with about 11 grams of sugar per serving which is already about half of the daily recommended sugar intake I had discussed earlier. But the

game's not over yet. Those vibrant packages you see lying on the market shelves today are loaded with even extra sugar.

Bonus Question- What about the yoghurts which are labeled as sugar free or with low sugar? Can we basically consume them in unlimited quantities? Try answering this after reading the chapter on artificial sugar.

2. Another risk factor is saturated fat. I know in the past topics, we basically discussed sugar as being the main culprit, but saturated fats are also not 100% innocent. They do a very good job in raising the bad cholesterol as I discussed in the comparison between the saturated fats and the trans fats. But the twilight on this dark night is that some yoghurts which are made of skimmed milk virtually have zero saturated fats in them. So it's always wise to check the labels for the saturated fat content.

Bonus Tip: Another benefit of checking the labels is getting to know whether the yoghurt is actually probiotic or not. As mentioned earlier, for yoghurt to be probiotic, it must have live bacteria inside it. All yoghurts contain live bacteria at some or the other point but if one of the processes in the preparation of yoghurt involving heating them is done faulty, no live bacteria would be present. One example of such yoghurts include the frozen yoghurts. So, you must look out for some sort of indications which explicitly call it probiotic.

3. Third reason yoghurts can backfire does not actually lie in the yoghurt. It lies inside you!

After reading the above benefits, it's not hard for anyone to just start eating yoghurt...because they just taste heavenly good. But the thing is they are made to taste good, so that onecup doesn't suffice you. Eating multiple cups of yogurt can actually cancel out all that good.

So hopefully, this should give you an insight about those slushy creamy-.

I had a slightly peculiar approach toward yoghurts. During weight loss, as far as I remember, I barely used to consume the packaged yogurt (like twice a week or so and that too when my mother bought it) just because I didn't want to add anything to what I am losing. But if you read the introduction part (if you didn't, then you must!), you must be knowing I had the genuine deadlines for me so that I can take part in a particular program. But one thing I did consume was the natural yoghurt made at home itself without any additives. Trust me, if you already consume that, just don't stop consuming that unless you want to miss the good things.

But if your taste buds just can't take it right now, I'd suggest you to first cut down the frequency of its consumption. Cut it to once per day if you had been consuming multiple of their servings per day. If you have been consuming it 7 days a week, bring it down to 2-3. Your main goal should be to reduce the frequency steadily and not make drastic changes which are analogous to short term goals. And whenever you get the chance to eat it, don't eat it in a rush: savor the moment. If you learn how to value the things you had been consuming recklessly, your consumption would automatically go down. One way to do that can be by not eating it while multitasking. You know, a friend of mine at school calls me Speedy, and it requires no further explanation: I just love speed. And if you're finding the idea of eating slowly counter- intuitive to saving time, let me do the job. So whenever I eat something which I know is high in calories, but my mind can't resist without it, I tend to take out time for it separately (for instance, taking out 5-10 minutes just for eating chips). One packet of chips contain approximately 400 calories (it's usually higher than 400 as a matter of fact). While I eat it, I'd taste and just try relating it to the spices that I have tasted before (one discovery I've made by doing this is that Haldiram's snack lite fries uses the taste maker that is very close to Maggie's magic masala!). I would go through the labels and have a 360 degree experience. So once I am done eating it, and whenever I would be craving for it again, I would envision it that it's there right in front me, rejuvenating my senses.

If you're still wondering how I save time over here, then take it this way: I save time by not having to do the exercise for the packet of chips, I just imagined eating. Burning 400 calories requires a 40 minute workout done at high intensity. So instead of piling up extra 400 calories and taking out time to increase my workout time, I'd rather just take out a fourth of that time by just enjoying what I eat! And this is not something I did just for losing weight, but rather I am doing for over a year even while maintaining my current weight. It's that simple :)

Chapter: 7

Zero Isn't Hero

I am not sure about you but have you ever got into an argument with someone over diet coke, where you're trying to explain that it does not contain any sugar since the label says it so, whereas the other person is sticking with his counter belief. In my case, I was the person sticking with the facts on its label. Most of us can relate to the dichotomy of the disguised individuals or the products: They appear to be sweet even though the "label" says it does not harm. Who should we trust, ourselves- the greatest creation of all times- or the manufacturers, who are bound to print "truth". With the "artificial sweeteners" becoming the buzz word of these days, there seem to be many facts which are hidden until this moment.

To start with, these substances are commonly referred to as "intense sweeteners", as they can be 1000 times sweeter than the regular sugar. And since most of us believe that all these fake sugars are bound to remain calorie-free, let me tell you: some of them actually do contain calories (of course, lesser than the regular sugar). And the reason they are virtually calorie-free is that they are made of chemicals our body just can't break up. So how do we perceive the sweetness? Well for that, I need to dig in biology. Our tongue consists of numerous cells, each having a certain kind of lock on its surface. As soon as we ingest some food, the particles of food act as a key that fit into these locks and trigger some response and that's how we feel the taste (these locks are analogous to insulin receptors discussed earlier in terms of mechanisms). Since we can easily distinguish between different tastes, it makes sense if I say that each taste also must have a certain unique lock and the sweet substances tend to fit in that lock perfectly. Now, as I have mentioned these fake sugars as disguised individuals, these substances have a shape similar to that of sugar, and hence they also trigger a similar response. So, that's what makes non sugars delightful and enough biology for now.

DOES IT HELP IN WEIGHT LOSS?

When I was on my weight loss program, I was very skeptical of drinking juices, so I refrained from actually drinking any at all. But there was this one bottle of lemonade which caught my attention with a big 'zero fat' mark on its cover. I initially wondered where it came from but it was too late for me to actually be able to take my eyes off that white beauty. I consoled myself and drank it. After that day, I didn't drink that for a while nor I really thought about it because of its overpriced tag, but my mum did get a bunch of bottles of it from a sale one day, which made me drink a bottle a day for at least two weeks. Did it end up helping me? Maybe.

But science doesn't really have a clear view on this. Some of the researchers seem to be supportive of these non-nutrient sweetened (NNS) beverages. One study conducted a 12-week study on individuals for whether having water carries some potential advantages over the NNS beverages in weight loss. The study showed that NNS drinkers actually showed greater reductions in feelings of hunger and had lost more weight. Another study compared effects of consumption of table sugar vs. artificially sweetened drinks on fat mass and energy levels and found out that table sugar beverages lead to increments in all of those parameters while such effects were not observed in the fake sugar group. But on the flip side, some researchers claim that the intake of these NNS products does not activate a pathway that leads to satisfaction and drags us to eating more of it. Logically, it also follows that it also makes our brain still feel hungry: just like we feel after drinking water. These researchers also claim that these additives also contribute to the increment of the hunger levels of the individuals.

So this matter is currently in debate, if it's fighting or fueling obesity. Looking back, I can tell that these sweeteners did help me divert my attention from other sugary cravings but only upto a certain threshold: until I got used to the flavor. After I got used to drinking the same lemon drink each and every single day, I could definitely tell that I was starting to become more inclined towards other sugary products but the urges were suppressible.

BACKFIRING OF THE SWEET PLAN:

I am sure the part must have been a moment of relief for most of us: after all, it's ZERO calories! But it's also essential to know the tricks our brain plays by making us believe that we are still under the control of our habits, where in fact, we're on the highway to hell.

We just discussed above that diet drinks don't necessarily have a negative impact on our weight loss programs since they don't increase blood sugar levels. But do you really expect that you can get all those sweet tastes without having to pay anything? Drinking these diet sodas makes us pay back in a slightly different currency. Instead of raising short term blood glucose levels, it **does** affect how our body would actually take in the regular sugar. Some of the studies have shown that artificial sweeteners lead to the development of insulin resistance (which increases the chances of type-2 diabetes) - when no more sugar can be taken up by our cells even after the secretion of insulin.

After reading this, my statements might seem to start looking contradictory in themselves: on one side I say it does not lead to the secretion of insulin, but on the other side it also contributes to the development of insulin resistance. I am not trying to create a fallacy over here. The reason for the two-sided argument is because there's already a splitted opinion. But let me also reiterate what happens in our body after its intake: our taste buds detect the sweet taste which puts our mind into a hypothetical energy boost state. However, this state is short-lived and as soon as the brian realizes the catch, it demands more of the real thing, like a puerile child.

There are a number of studies on the psychological impact of this stage. One experiment included 115 undergraduates who were served one of the 3 available beverages without telling them the distinctions: sprite, sprite zero, lemon-lime flavored sparkling drinking water. Then, they were shown 3 items: M&Ms, Trident sugar-free gum, and natural spring water.

Researchers found that those who consumed the sprite zero were 2.93 more likely to go for M&Ms (the highest sugar content food)!

CONSUME OR NOT TO CONSUME: We have just figured it out that our brain makes us more likely to pick up a high energy item after the ingestion of the NNS drink. It comes with no surprise that this may be a possible hindrance towards our ultimate goal.

Personally, I have heard and read stories from people where some of them actually find zero drinks as an opportunity to avoid the sugary drinks and others who actually feel addicted to it and are actively looking for ways to overcome it. So all this comes down to is one phenomena: self experimentation.

Another reason to avoid is that the over-stimulation of our sugar receptors makes us want to increase the dose every single time. This also means that it becomes harder and harder to switch over to drinks like green tea which actually helps in fat dissolution.

Whether you are one of the addicted ones or the usual drinkers, stopping to drink it would most likely be a positive change: after all, it's more natural.

BRINGING THE CHANGE:

Before even trying, most of us have our excuses ready: 'We have a sweet tooth'. I get it, no big deal. The only big deal is if you are willing to bring in the change or not. Just demonstrating the willingness means you have won 52% of the battle. For the rest, I will help you out.

You must have watched those famous Nicotine chewing gum ads which have led to the evolution of new classroom jokes. But jokes apart; if we try to bridge the similarities, drinking diet sodas is an addiction just like smoking. The chewing gums displayed in those ads aren't the ordinary chewing gums: they have the same taste as what a smoker would taste with those deadly tobacco buds: just a non-lethal alternative. In a similar way, choosing yet another alternative for the sweeteners is using natural sugars: the ones available in the fruits. The way for it is by preparing detox water: submerging sliced fruit in the potable water and drinking it after a couple of hours. I have read numerous stories of people wanting something more than the water, and the detox water does the job just well.

The first time I tried detox water, I totally fell in love with it. I did get used to the stimulus after a couple of days, but it did the job: bringing down the sugar cravings. Also, one is always welcome to get creative in adding different permutations and combinations of fruits to the water.

Once you're set on detox, you can take further steps by moving on to various teas: green, lemon, black. I have been drinking these teas for a couple of years from now, so I actually crave these teas now.

Before you vilify these NNS drinks anymore, consider this statement by Osama Hamdy, director of the inpatient diabetes program at Harvard's Joslin Diabetes Center: "Although it's just an association — which means it is not the cause — I personally don't recommend [drinking diet sodas], as they change intestinal microbiota," he says. "[But] if you ask me to choose between sugar-sweetened beverages and diet sodas, I will choose diet sodas."

Chapter: 8

Being Hooked On Sugar

By now, we have talked a lot about sugar, and I am sure if you see this coming up again,you'd dread to hear about it again. And I totally agree with that too. But, there is one more aspect to it, and if that's left untouched, there's no point in what we have explored so far. Let me bring my mother in this picture, to explain what it is. Now of course, I have been telling her facts about how bad sugar is, quite for some time, but she just can't avoid it: Her sweet consumption hasn't fluctuated even a little. You must have guessed the problem by now: SUGAR ADDICTION. This situation is analogous to that of the people who are very well aware of the devastating effects of smoking but still can't resist it. And let me bring it up right now: This condition is much more serious than you think. So this is something to read carefully.

Let me start by explaining what sugar addiction actually is.

Have you ever been offered a deal by your parents, in which you would get chocolate you die for, in return for getting good grades or something similar? And then on hearing the deal, you would actually start working towards it and go beyond boundaries to get it done. I have been offered such deals but not in return

for chocolates because I never desired them more than the crunchy spicy wafers! But anyway, when you get the chocolate, it marks a sense of achievement you just accomplished. And that's the exact same way your brain treats it: something to be cherished more and more. Be it the moments of joy or grief, we tend to offer sweets literally to anyone irrespective of their identity, background, etc. And, in our daily lives, we tend to use the word "Addiction" in much less devastating situations, say, for example being addicted to "Clash of Clans" or sometimes a sport. But in the terms of medicine, experts describe Addiction as a "tragic situation in which someone's brain chemistry has been altered to compel them to repeat a substance or an activity despite its harmful consequences." So basically, sugar addiction can be like drug addiction. In fact, researchers have shown that sugar addiction can be more addictive than that of Cocaine's!

But how on Earth is that possible? For that, we need to understand how we get addicted in the first place and what are its general consequences. There's this neurotransmitter in our brain called dopamine which is an integral part of the "Reward Circuit" and hence is associated with addictive behavior. If a certain action causes excessive dopamine release, we feel immense happiness and also a strong surge to repeat the action. But due to the repetition of the activity, our brain automatically adjusts by suppressing the dopamine levels. So logically, the only way to be able to achieve the dopamine level of the same extent as before is by repeating the task but with a higher dosage, and perhaps with higher frequency, so as to achieve that level. And every time you repeat the task, it needs to be of a higher dose than the previous one, leading to substance abuse. In the case of sugar, it activates opiate receptors in our brain which interfere with the reward circuit and hence make us crave for it even after the knowledge of the consequences like weight gain, headaches, etc. A study done in 2008 by Princeton University found out that under certain conditions, rats could become dependent and addicted to sugar as they showed symptoms like binge eating, craving, and withdrawal. And answering why sugar addiction can be more dangerous than drug addiction; sugar addiction also interferes with our stress hormones. Another reason why it is so hard to get rid of this addiction is that sugar is something that is much more socially acceptable, than, say, alcohol or drugs.

If you feel like you're one of the victims of it, there are, in fact, a number of things you can do.

First of all, just don't go straight ahead to a no-sugar diet since that is virtually impossible to sustain. Instead, I want you to go in baby steps by making slight changes that you actually forget the difference in about a week. Another thing you can do is to reduce the quantity of added sugar you were taking. For example, in my case, I used to drink milk with 2 spoons of sugar added in it, daily. After learning the dark nature of sugar, I didn't completely stop adding sugar or drinking milk at all. Instead, for 2 weeks, I cut those 2 spoons to 1, and after that, I stopped consuming it at all. This way my taste buds easily adapted to the plain milk flavor, and now I even find the plain milk sweet for some reasons.

The main thing I want you to understand is that sugar is a part of our basic diet and staying away from it completely is not an option. But changing the influx quantity and rate is all we can do and must do!

Chapter: 9

The Unheard Cries

It's a big day, today: the day for a test. In the past, you had heard about chocolates being a brain booster, so you decided to continuously binge on those brown bars. Perhaps you took that fact way too seriously. Walking through the hallways of the examination building, you see kids scattered in groups and all you hear is the anxiety and fast flipping of the pages. You make your way through,without making eye contact and you see your allotted room, finally. While taking out your needed stationery, you don't really see any symptoms of hyperactivity, but your lips are constantly forming words, saying that chocolate boost will work at the right time. You step into the room, sit down and prepare as the test sheets are being handed over. But hold on, you just realize that the matters are not getting any better and in fact, the deviation is only negative after starting the test.

What had just happened over there? Was it that you were underprepared? Not likely, since you do your part well. But the problem must have been somewhere or how did you miss what you'd wished for? Coming out of fantasy, my whole point for this 200-word imagery was to bust one of the myths that 'more chocolate=better performance.'

If you have been keeping a track of the terms I have been using lately, then talking about insulin resistance again shouldn't be new. And the main point of the above discussion was to direct your attention to the symptoms of insulin resistance. Controlled intake is fine, but I am going to start from what happens to our brain and learning power if we develop insulin resistance.

The condition that the "you" character had during the test is self- explanatory: negative. But how?

Insulin resistance interferes with the clean-up process of the proteins in the brain. If this clean-up process does not take place, it leads to serious conditions like impairment in learning and also Alzheimer's disease, which is caused by the accumulation of these proteins. It also forms the base of other neurodegenerative diseases like Parkinson's.

And another misconception that might arise at this point is that these symptoms wouldn't be visible before diabetes. But, studies have shown that the deteriorating effects of insulin resistance can be seen even years before one develops diabetes.

This problem is serious and hard to let go as discussed in the chapter on sugar addiction.

Chapter: 10

Supplements That Dont Quite Supplement

When I had met with an accident in 2009, I was bedridden, give or take for 10 months. I wasn't able to walk without a walker and also wasn't able to eat regular food. I was strictly asked to stay away from any sweets because of my minimal physical movement. I recovered and in a couple of months, things turned out to be normal again. But, one morning before I was leaving for my morning school, I saw a big greenish-grey colored tablet kept next to my glass of milk. It wouldn't have been a big deal had I not taken such a high number of tablets when I was on bed rest. Thoughts raced through my mind wondering if I was still under supervision and if I was still not normal.

Before I could think of anything else, I had started walking towards my mother who was working in another corner of the house. I approached her and looked at her face with the tablet in my hand. Perhaps, she might have comprehended what I had intended to say since I still hadn't formed words when she said, "This will help you get the nutrients you had missed earlier."

The next question I could think of was if it was prescribed by the doctor. As soon as she replied in negative, a sense of relief started flowing in my mind. Without a second thought, I declined the offer and ran straight to the school. I did realize it was a multi-nutrient tablet by Amway, but my decision didn't fluctuate even in the upcoming days. Thankfully, she stopped asking me to consume it after a while.

Fast-forwarding to 2019, my grandma had a fracture and the primary reason for this was the lack of calcium. She had recovered (thankfully) but my mum again started to offer me those dull tablets, and for some reason, I did fall for them ; however, this lasted only for a week. My mind just couldn't agree on taking some nutrients in the form of some tablets because I had formed an association that taking tablets means that things are not going as planned.

Luckily, while I was looking for content for this book, I also ran into a course that talked on supplements. And as soon as I saw this word, I heaved a sigh of relief since this was something I was so curious to know about.

WHAT ARE SUPPLEMENTS

If this feels like a foreign word to you, let me first introduce it. In a Harvard article, Sus Farrell, MD, Director of the comprehensive clinical skills OSCE examination at Harvard Medical School, has said that supplements include, "Herbal or complementary products, and vitamin or amino acid micronutrients." And yes, you read the word "herbal", right.

As more and more people are trying to be in their best possible form, the exercise and good diet are now gradually starting to become more of a novice term again. And thanks to the intense advertisement by the industrialists which have spread a decent word about the potential pluses of such products, but no one has really talked about the minuses. Fthe record, the name of the article whose author I have quoted above wrote the article about these supplements with the title, "Harmful effects of supplements can send you to the emergency department."!

By now it must have been clear to all that the old saying of 'more the merrier,' doesn't exactly hold true for the body. But since this saying has been much instilled in our cultural backgrounds, we always tend to promote the positive feedback loop but fail to apply the negative one; mostly when those habits have been ingrained inside us.

Anyway, to give you an idea of exactly how many people are affected by these counterfeit nutrients, a study in the United States found out that there are as many as 23,000 emergency department visits per year just because of the supplement ingestions. Out of this high number, 28% of the people included young adults ranging from 20-34 of age. The average age of the patients was 32 and more than half of the patients included women. This disparity was also seen in the group of people affected by some specific supplements. For example, more women were affected by supplements that were dedicated to weight loss, and the majority of the people affected by the bodybuilding supplements were men.

NEGATIVE EFFECTS OF TAKING SUPPLEMENTS: The same research I discussed above also found out that more than half of the cases were caused by supplements for weight loss. These weight loss supplements were also the major cause of cases involving cardiac symptoms. In fact, there were more cases of cardiac symptoms from the intake of weight loss (43%) and energy (46%) supplements than from the stimulants (23%). And to make matters worse, stimulants always come with warning signs on their labels but you would never find one on those on the supplements.

Vitamin and anti-oxidant supplementations don't have the fairy-tale effects either. For instance, vitamin E administered to reduce vascular diseases (like periphery artery disease, carotid artery disease, etc.) does not actually suppress these events. And artificial antioxidants can even increase the mortality rate.

I could go on and on to elucidate numerous other cases where things don't go as intended but these examples should be enough to set the base.

CASES WHEN YOU DO REQUIRE SUPPLEMENTS: There are always exceptions to the rules, however. Some of the high-risk groups can actually benefit from taking supplements.

For instance, people who're suffering from osteoporosis (decrease of bone density) need to have an intake of some extra vitamin D and calcium for coping up. Another very common group who has to take these calcium and vitamin D supplements include lactose intolerants who can't derive those nutrients from their diet. People who are genetically designed to absorb less of some nutrients will also be under the high-risk groups.

I remember after my grandma came back from the hospital, she was also supposed to consume some of the supplements, including calcium.

Regardless of all, googling up your symptoms in order to identify if you're included in one of the high-risk groups would also make you plan for your upcoming funeral. Seriously! This is the exact mistake I made when the diet I followed went wrong (which I would discuss in this chapter). Google would provide you with extreme cases like cancer and whatnot, so, the best thing to do is....go to a qualified doctor, please.

Similar to the artificial vs. natural sugar case we had discussed earlier, over here as well, the natural turns out to be superior to the artificial in terms of the nutrients. A study tested the hypothesis of whether a high intake of natural nutrients triggers an inflammatory response. For this, they gave the participants a carotenoid rich diet and divided the participants into 3 groups based on their quantity of intake: 2, 5, 8 serving a day. Upon examination, they found that high consumption increased the carotenoid concentration in blood plasma without triggering any inflammatory response, indicating that the natural is always welcomed in our body.

Supplements aren't for whimsical targets, and the need for supplements doesn't require being expeditious when the organic sources contain plenty of nutrients as a whole.

Chapter: 11
Ideal World

We have uncovered the mystery of culprits; discussed on sugars, artificial sugars, supplements, etc. But there still remains one big fat unanswered question: What is the ideal diet? After discussing and figuring out all the negative foods, finding the gems now shouldn't be that big of a deal.

About 3-4 years ago, there was this new diet system that came to my mother's knowledge: NO MILK RAW DIET. She had heard it from her peers and their workshop claimed that losing weight would be a cake walk. I heard it and decided to attend their workshop because, at the back of my mind, I knew I was a 'bit' obese.

And this was not the first time I had heard about a "diet that worked" case, I had asked from pretty much everyone in my links, who had lost weight, but it just wouldn't work. Even so, everyone who saw me after I had lost weight would ask me the things that I had done, in the hope to decipher the formula they can apply. I am repeating myself over that each one of us is UNIQUE. And as cliché as it may sound, this is the point which the most miss. Even my mother, who tried to trail my path, couldn't cope up with it and could only make it to a fraction of her desired goal.

My goal for this section is to talk about 3 of the most popular diets which, I believe, successful weight losers must have incorporated in their lifestyles at some point. Again, there would be absolutely no need to follow one of those diets strictly because it just wouldn't work. Instead, your goal should be to identify some general trends in these diets: what's the core concept each diet focuses on, and identify the range of food you have to be within the limits of (in the range, you must also identify the maximum and minimum, i.e. the food you can eat any time at one end and the food which you could rarely afford to eat).Once you have a grasp over this trend, you can make some new novel combinations and create an entirely new system on your own!

The first and one of the most popular diets is the **Mediterranean diet**. Now, this diet is my personal favorite diet since my food choices majorly revolved around this. I have included the food pyramid for the same below which is arranged in the decreasing order of their significance: with foods to be included in every meal at the bottom to the rare foods for intake at the top.

As it is clearly visible, the foods with the least priority are meat and the added sugars. To study the effects of this diet, a study was performed which turned out to be a landmark study. In this, they provided all the participants with the Med diet and one other substance: either nuts, or low-fat diet, or the olive oil. All three groups took similar components of the med pyramid, including fruits, veggies, etc. The results showed that those on the olive oil or nuts had a higher cognition than the low-fat dieters and also had reduced risks of cardiovascular disease. This was indeed a landmark study since it again reinforces the fact that fats are not the culprit and also shows the novel nature of the Med diet.

If you're wondering which group amongst the two reaped the maximum points, it is the Med diet + nuts (I have included these in my academic papers as well). The study from which I took the data discussed that both the cases should have had profound effects in reducing obesity, depression, but the nut combination just turned out to be relatively better.

Have you ever heard the person's thinking capability starting to deteriorate as he ages? Well, this diet is very efficient in preventing that from happening. Another way it stops the ill effects of aging is by delaying the aging of the cell itself by reducing oxidative stress. So be it memory, learning, depression, obesity, or aging, this diet would have you covered.

But again, you don't have to follow this diet word to word. I would recommend you to look into the foods off the chart that can be made available to you and then tailor the program accordingly. Personally, being a vegetarian, I didn't consume fish and sea food, wine, or meat. After you have figured out the availability, start writing down the foods in range as I have discussed before. Make sure to actually write down what you intend to eat more frequently and put a very clear symbol against foods you intend to eat only after a certain interval, like sweets. In my range, I had the usual vegetables and fruits in the bottom row as regular eating, 2 cookies of Oreos on every alternative day, and shallow fried Indian cuisines like *Parathas* once a week. And even though the Med diet recommends yoghurt intake weekly, I used to have it twice every week. Talking about the very high-calorie foods like pizza or Indian *Tikki*, I made sure to not have them more than once every 1.5 months - 2 months, at least. I also had set a big No-No to the chips since that was something I used to be addicted to.

The second diet I am going to discuss is the **Ketogenic Diet**, also known as a low carb, high-fat diet. This diet recommends an insane amount of fats with the breakdown as follows: 70% fat, 20% proteins, and 10% carbs. And 10% carbs doesn't mean 10% only from the sugar; this includes carbs coming from veggies and the starchy fruits. To have a better idea how it looks like, just invert the Mediterranean diet pyramid.

On a Keto Diet, you get your calories from animal sources, olives, coconuts, avocados, eggplant, onion, garlic, etc. And, you would get the proteins from eggs,and fruit intake would be limited to that of berries, and other low carb fruits.

I am personally not a big fan of this diet for a couple of reasons. Number one, this encourages animal-based fat intake which is not the best source to derive our nutrients from, for every single day. Secondly, it limits our fruit intake which is rich in basal nutrients.

However, this may be a very useful diet to follow in case one develops insulin resistance or in treating diabetes. Another big plus point of ketosis is that it helps in the reduction of toxic proteins leading to Alzheimer's. This could be shown through a study in which rats were fed with the keto diet had a lesser amount of toxic proteins than the rats on the standard diet. It is also known to alleviate the conditions in other neurodegenerative diseases like Parkinson's (symptoms include tremors and other physical impairments). This was shown in a human trial, where patients who were suffering from Parkinson's were kept on a keto diet and were observed for 28 days. Patients showed drastic improvements ranging from 20 to even 80%!

However, since the majority of the teens don't encounter these issues, sticking to the Med diet, in this case, might be a viable option.

The last type of diet which is again my personally preferred diet is the **Intermittent Fasting**. And the reason I really admire this diet is that you can incorporate this diet simultaneously with any other diet: just like dual citizenships. The basic concept of this diet is eating food in a specified window and not eating anything outside that time window. And.....that's it!

It does not specifically require you to eat any particular foods but focuses only and only on the food timings, which is easier said than done.

As the name suggests, this definitely must involve some hours of the day when you are not consuming anything except water. And that number is 16. You would be having your full day's meal in 8 hours and not eat for the next 16 hours. Before you start panicking, the good news is the number of sleep hours also count in the period of fasting: since you're not eating anything, right?

Since I am a huge fan of intermittent fasting, I still follow it with minimal deviations. This involves eating my dinner at 7-7:30

pm, not eating anything before going to bed, and then eating my first meal in the morning between 10-11 am. You might notice the number of hours of my fasting may not accurately add to 16 hours, which is totally fine. You can come with your own combination like 15-9 or 20-4. And if you're wondering if the water is the only thing you're allowed to take in the fasting period, then that's not exactly the case. Anything less than 50 calorie intake still counts in fasting mode. So, you can be a bit more creative and also make yourself some nice tea or coffee. But beware of nuts and almonds since they might appear small but they definitely have more than 50 calories. As long as the fasting hours exceed at least 13 hours, it should be good.

But you may ponder that if there isn't any calorie restriction, how is even that helpful? One of the biggest plus points of this type of fasting is the changes in hormones (like insulin) it produces which wouldn't be as pronounced via a simple calorie deficient diet. And these hormonal changes could be used to reverse the insulin resistance symptoms without much aid (of course, combining a diet with intermittent fasting would be a more effective way).

Still, it's hard to make sense that we can see charismatic benefits just by adjusting the food timings. So, an iso-caloric study was conducted in which participants in 2 groups received an equal number of calories initially, but one group was put on intermittent fasting and another on calorie restriction. The researchers monitored the insulin levels of both the groups and found significant differences. Initially, both the groups had a drop of insulin levels, but later, the insulin levels plateaued for the calorie restriction group. The intermittent fasting group continued to see the drop in the insulin. This proves that this type of fasting will produce unique effects which calorie restriction one does not, and plays a major role in taking the insulin sensitivity back to normal.

Tracing back the evolutionary relationships with our ancestors, Intermittent fasting mimics the way our ancestors used to eat their food: in periods of food availability with intermittent famines.

In order to see its relationships with the brain and check which sort of fasting can be proven to be most beneficial, researchers designed an experiment in which one group of mice was kept on intermittent fasting, other on a keto diet, with the standard diet as the control. The intermittent fasting mice performed the best, followed by mice on a keto diet, and the standard diet mice at the end. These results are also proved valid on humans as well.

I hope these 3 classical diets should give you a sense of how to improve the diet when on a weight loss program. But it is important to take note that there are numerous diets around us. To give you a sense of the variations, let me share a bit from what I learnt from the NO MILK RAW DIET workshop I had attended. They said that these days, cows are given drugs and other doses to increase the yield of the milk extracted from them.

While this may be true, the bonuses one might be missing from it are just too hard to compensate from other forms. The logic behind the raw diet was that cooking actually destroys nutrients, so having them raw ensures their preservation. But the research shows that cooking or boiling food actually ensures their better absorption in the body with most of the nutrients being retained. No doubt, some of the nutrients are lost like vitamin C, and we can minimize the loss by following a couple of steps: consuming the water in which the vegetables were cooked, peeling the vegetables only after cooking, using less water, etc.

The workshop organizers even came up with some sort of vegetable juice which tasted like spicy *Gol Gappa pani*, which I found intriguing. There were also other dishes like raw mixed veggie *poha*, which didn't appeal my senses to that extent. And to be honest, I did end up losing like 5 kg in a short amount of time, but I just found it to be unsustainable. As fast I had lost weight, it wasn't very long that I noticed the weighing needle reverse its direction to where it was for the past years. These radical changes are hard to incorporate in our daily routines. Rather, if we just analyze and keep a track of our current diet and make some recombinations in it, we can come up with a diet on which we would have complete control.

Lastly, only focusing on the diet wouldn't be enough. Without physical activity, you wouldn't reach the threshold required to start losing weight. Take another look at the bottom text of the Med diet food pyramid.

Chapter: 12

Slow And Steady Wins ... Seriously

It was November 1st 2018 when I had started my weight loss program. I set my calorie intake limit to 2100 and started recording every food that I ate on the My Fitness Pal app. I was also mindful of what I eat, for the first time in my life. As the day went by, I made sure to record my meal right with full accuracy: to correct quantity and type. I didn't stop myself from eating regular food, but I also made sure that I don't eat any chips to avoid overshooting on my very first day. By the end of the day, I saw the number 2300 flashing right at me. This depicted the number of calories I had taken throughout the day which included everything from the milk I drank to the meals I ate. "I have to cut it down," was the first thought that popped right after I saw these 4 digits. I remember going to the maximum calorie intake settings and adjusting it to 1800 from the earlier 2000; I knew in my mind that I can't let it go above the limit.

I followed the usual routine by keeping track of the meals that I ate on the second day as well, and I also increased my salad intake and avoided eating bread rolls that I had devoured the previous day. And as the day went by with the number of allowed calories kept decreasing, I noticed something special: As soon as I tracked my Workout on the app, the number of calories I burnt was added to the number of calories of my daily allowance. Believe me or not, I saw this as a "hack"; the more I exercise, the more I am allowed to eat. That day I had +150 calories of the day, that is, I had performed better by having 150 calories in my balance.

My fight with calories eased, and I started finding the 1800 target not a deadline target anymore. So, I went ahead and reduced it to 1600, and making this goal obsolete too wasn't a tough job either. I kept reducing my calorie intake goal and also started to cut my food intake when I couldn't fit in any more workouts aside from the calories burnt by the staircase I was climbing.

And…guess what, there was one time I had set my goal to 600 calories where I would try to eat around 450-500 calories and also workout so in the end, so I had like +600 calories, as if I had not eaten that day. This became like a new game for me where I would try to set a new high score of the calories remaining by eating less and exercising more. There was a day when I even had +1000 calories left!

But, what I did was a terribly misguided approach. Cutting the body's calorie intake to such drastic levels would be a fatal mistake. But, consider this point- it makes sense to cut down to lose weight, right? The lesser you eat those calories,the lesser fat is going to get accumulated. This is true, but the extremes do not produce novel results. I can vividly describe the consequences I faced later due to this restricted diet.

Initially, things seemed to be in equilibrium, roughly until January- with just 2 months into dieting. I vividly remember the first time I started to face these symptoms was when I was preparing for my board exams. As I was doing my work, I felt some pain build up in my upper stomach area. I tried to ignore it since my friends were already calling me to the park. But, things didn't really improve. There seemed to be an exponential growth in the intensity of pain in a matter of minutes, and I just couldn't stand anymore. I felt my body ,as if, on fire. That fire was only extinguished by the warm water which my grandma gave me. And ironically, the intensity of the pain went down with the same rate it went up, and within minutes, I was already playing in the park. I thought about it, discussed it with my friend, and then forgot about it in a day or so. Little did I know that this was just the beginning of what was about to happen with me later.

One of the very common consequences of cutting down the calories is **a decrease in the metabolism**: less of the nutrient influx will be converted to energy (as low as just 23%) and will be used more for storage. And what's worse: the metabolism will remain low even after we stop calorie restriction for a considerable amount of time. Because of this, even if you reach your goal weight, you're more likely to regain the weight as the research states as many as 80% of the individuals do regain it (seems like I was in the minority).

But the loss of metabolism is just hay in the stack. Other things you might have to face is the loss in **muscle mass, fatigue due to lack of nutrients,** etc. The muscle mass is lost primarily due to the lack of proteins in the diet. So, the muscles could be retained if we ingest protein through some external sources like protein powder and do resistance training. Even though I did severe calorie restriction, I definitely took protein powder and used to do skipping(a resistance training) every day combined with occasional running which might have helped me retain my muscles.

Unfortunately, it's not just the proteins that you may be missing by severe calorie restriction. There are several other nutrients that our body gets deprived of and can even lead to irregular heart rhythms, hair loss, increased fracture risk, or permanent eye damage. And we already know that carbs are the bad boys we all trying to get rid of, but severe deprivation from carbs also can lead to fatigue in some Individuals. However, I remember when I was on severe calorie restriction, I never really felt any symptoms of fatigue, rather my body was relatively more active than it was on the usual diet. And the research actually supports this idea: Each body is different and may respond differently. Low carb diet in some individuals can actually decrease fatigue and actually may lead to better retention of the diet.

After the first pain attack, I was doing just fine for a couple of days. One afternoon, I had eaten some homemade pizza pockets, and my other family members had left for somewhere in the evening. I had plans to just continue my preparations for the test, but little did I know what was going to happen. Now I am not going to lie, I was having a very mild stomach ache before anyone left, but it was something I could easily ignore. After 30 minutes or so, that stomach ache started to grow at the same place and pace, and within minutes, I was back on my bed. I wasn't able to think much except for the past encounter, and perhaps some thermal energy of water could ironically again extinguish the exponentially growing flames. I somehow got up and went to the kitchen, heated some water, and drank it in one go. As I gulped down the water, my entire concentration was diverted to the upper stomach area looking for symptoms of relief. But I couldn't notice the sweat drops slowing down as they had earlier.

I could only feel the matter getting worse and the next thing that could come to my mind was taking Carom seeds (Ajwain) as that's what I used to take in any stomach related problem since childhood. The only problem was I just didn't know where it was. With the energy I had, I tried some of my final efforts which turned out to be futile. But I have to mention it again that the pain was just so horrendous that I thought this is the end. My body was on fire again and even though it was winter, I just couldn't wear that jacket anymore. I lied down and tried calling my mother but you know, when the time's against you, matters only get worse: yeah, she didn't pick up. It also seemed like my pain had developed some sort of resistance against laying down such that even laying straight couldn't bring me any relief like it had in the past. It turns out I was saved that night since I somehow managed to reach my neighbors who were kind enough to help me out.

But this wasn't the peak of these surging flames either. The problem was that my metabolism had reduced to such an extent that it just became impossible for me to eat anything heavier than my body had become adapted to. I started having mild problems even after I ate just two chapatis. And every time it would happen, it would develop the resistance for the previous thing that curbed it. After a couple of months we found that I had some sort of bacterial infection for which I had to take antibiotics for 3 months straight.

And, this brings me to the next side effect of a severe calorie deficit diet which is **Lower Immunity.** As I experienced in my case, a number of research studies have found out that the athletes who attempted to lose weight were more likely to be sick in the following 3 months of the event. However, this link is not direct for non-exercising individuals.

WHAT'S THE LIMIT TO THE CALORIE RESTRICTION: I hope I was clear enough that the limit to the calorie restriction shouldn't approach zero. But what is it then?

The truth is that there's no objective answer. It could be 1400 for someone, 1200 or even 1800-2000. There are a number of factors on which it depends on age, height, weight, gender, and physical activity. The easiest way I can think of to determine the optimum calorie intake level is by using online calculators which can give you a fairly good sense of your calorie intake relative to your current goals: maintaining weight, losing weight, intense weight loss, etc.

One useful resource is calculator.net in which if you go over the health and fitness calculator and choose the calorie calculator option, you can get a sense of your calorie intake.

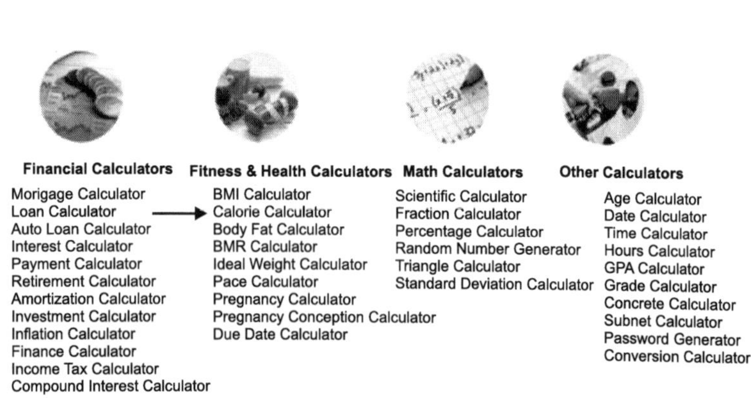

For testing, I entered my details and here are the results for the same:

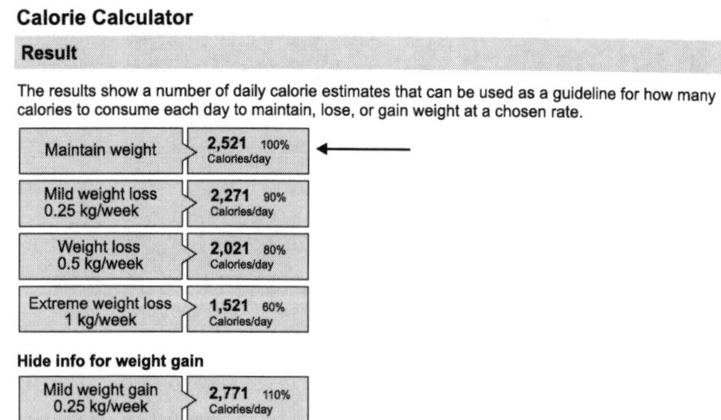

Now, of course, I will ignore the weight gain part and focus only on maintaining weight which shows 2521 calories. To be honest, I was a bit baffled by such a high number since even on my first day of weight loss, I ate around 2200 calories, and after I had stopped losing weight, I also stopped tracking myself: since I found it to be more intrinsic. So, I decided to calculate my day's calorie intake and I found out that I ate, give or take, 2300 calories, which was about what I was expected to eat. And this has been my diet ever since I recovered from my illness.

Another source that can help you give a sense of the ideal calorie intake is My Fitness Pal app (this app told me to take 2500 calories, so both the sources are reliable). Since I used this app to track all of my meals, exercises, I have added an extensive explanation over its usage in the weight loss chapter.

MIDDLE PATH RULE APPLIES OVER HERE AS WELL

After I have mentioned quite a few times throughout this book that following the middle path is the best way possible, and this rule works well over here too. Now if I do a quick calculation, taking my past weight, to check the appropriate amount of calories for extreme weight loss, it advises me going to a minimum of 1190 calories with a little side note of caution:

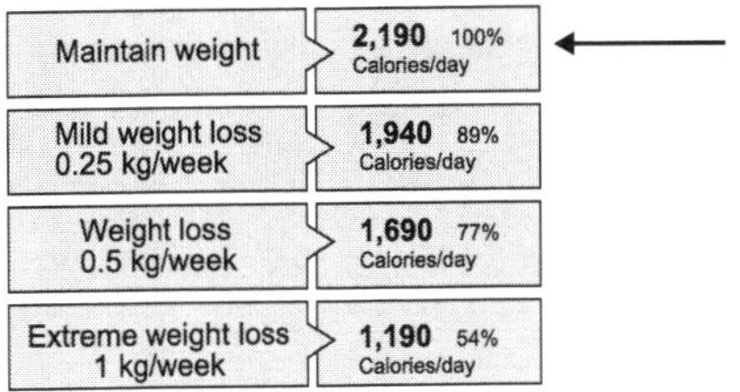

Had I stuck to these numbers, there were numerous advantages I could have enjoyed. Let me pour down a couple of those. Firstly, it helps **increase the verbal memory** by as much as by 20%. A study was conducted where 50 adults were classified into 3 groups: the calorie restrictor, increased unsaturated fatty acid consumers (but no change in total fat intake by decreasing the saturated fatty acid consumption), and no change group. Only the calorie restriction group showed improvements. Not only does it increase the memory, it also prevents cognitive decline by bringing down the insulin levels. Some studies have also reported that it shows anti-aging effects as well.

It might be safe to assume that these benefits of calorie restriction are expressed only while losing weight, right? Nope. One study analyzed the effects of 25% calorie deficit diets on metabolic health in already fit individuals (with BMI ranging from 22-27.9). They kept a track of the participants starting from May 2007 to February 2010. However, not everyone could keep up with the 25% calorie deficits; all of them at least did it up to 12%. They examined the individuals and found that they have shown a remarkable improvement. All of them had reduced proteins which are an indicator of inflammation linked heart disease, cancer, and cognitive decline. This study indicates that you will be already enjoying the calorie deficit boost even before you start losing weight.

After going through a roller coaster journey especially with dieting, where I felt helpless even in the middle of my board exams and on the day of the exam, switching through pills every time, calling my family doctor. I would have never done the extremes if I had known this would happen before. I would never want any of the readers of this book to go through that so I had to write this crucial part.

Takeaways

1. Macros we consume don't stay in their definitive form, for instance proteins and carbs taken in can easily be converted to fats and soon be visible around our belly. Hence, it's imperative to eat in moderation.
2. Fats are the ones that receive all criticism because they are the only ones which act as the physical indicator of our erratic lifestyle. The fact is that Intaking of excessive carbs and leading a sedentary lifestyle is the primary cause of obesity since extra carbs are stored in our body as fats.
3. Having insulin's support is must for weight loss as this is the one that prevents conversion of carbs into fats and knocks on every cell's door to take in that carb.
4. Too much insulin makes cells resistant to its knocks. Say hello to diabetes.
5. Eating fruits is healthy because they have a lower glycemic index which prevents rapid upsurge in the insulin levels. Foods rich in fiber have a lower glycemic index.
6. Consumption of food rich in omega 3, like fatty acid-fish, flax seeds, nuts, is helpful as this is the compound which our body can't make.
7. Limit the intake of food rich in saturated fats-red meat, butter, ice cream. Avoid consumption of trans fats at any cost- Fast foods, chips, crackers, and cookies. These are the most malicious of all.
8. Plant based proteins fulfils our body's requirements better than animal proteins. However, throwing in animal protein occasionally is actually beneficial.
9. Processing of food actually cuts down all the essentials that the food was born with, making it only desirable

for the shelf. Salads may look more expensive than those creamilicious assassins but in terms of cost per nutrient, they are much cheaper! Therefore, change the lens with which you view that natural entity.

10. For a person consuming 2000 calories, only 25g of sugar is considered safe or 4 teaspoons. Since everything we lay our eyes on these days has sugar; it's imperative for us to avoid adding guilt to it by eating all those cookies, ice creams as much as possible.
11. Companies try to disguise the sugar content by using various synonyms for it.
12. Drinking fresh extracted juice from homemade fruits could produce almost same detrimental result in the body as one of those packaged juices because the fiber is stripped out from it. Fibers are what make fruit a friend and not foe.
13. If you're not lactose intolerant, enjoy dairy products. Some types of yoghurts-like greek yoghurt- are actually beneficial.
14. Taking artificial sugar can backfire because eating artificial sugar like showing a genetically sweet toothed baby, pictures of chocolate. Like the baby starts craving those chocolates even more, so does our body. Net result? Negative.
15. Sugar addiction exists and is even stronger than cocaine addiction. Taking baby steps is the best way possible to annihilate sugar addiction without coming under the suspect radar of our sugar addicted mind.
16. Anything unnatural is not desirable. While supplements can aid some individuals who are severely in need of it, replacing natural foods with supplements doesn't work.
17. In order to find the best diet, first analyze what you currently eat and make changes accordingly. Divide all your dishes into 3 categories: meals you can have anytime,

moderate amounts, or to be avoided at any costs. Increase the frequency of anytime meals and try replacing the 3rd category foods with-roughly-equally mouth watering and relatively healthier options. For instance, replacing pizza with Papdi Chaat (which I did).

18. Mediterranean diet is considered one of the best diets for losing weight. Keto diet may be good for individuals suffering from diabetes.
19. Intermittent fasting is one of the best things of all you can do with absolutely no efforts. Just have a time lag of around 15 hours between your evening and next morning meal and voila: FREE FAT BURN GUARANTEED. This will suit almost anyone because that's how our ancestors ate their meals.
20. Middle path is the best path. Extreme calorie restriction can be significantly disastrous, talking from first hand perspective. On the other hand, moderate calorie restriction has benefits like delayed aging, and even improving our grades!

Module 2

EXERCISE PILL

Chapter: 1
Introduction

"Even after being acquainted with the cliched saying "Exercise makes us healthy", there has been no decline in the increase of sedentarism all across the globe. Not wanting to practice healthy goals isn't the root cause here, but rather, it's more about the result of yet another cause.

As per Google, the term 'fitness' seems to be much more widely used in the contemporary world than in the 90s era. However, this doesn't qualify it as a modern evolution.

Ever since the dawn of man, physical development was more of an innate quality, which ensured the survival and social interactions. Phrases like "Run for your life" could be used to reflect the link between life and physical activities like running, be it to break out of peril circumstances, or mundane activities like hunting, which wouldn't be possible without locomotive skills.

Between 10,000 and 8000 BC, agriculture became another driver towards bodily actions. This provides an insight that people at that time weren't driven to follow the path of physical fitness; rather, it was intrinsic.

Between 4000 BC and the fall of the Roman Empire in 476 AD, their motives began to shape to a level above their mere existence: to conquer. Assyrians, Babylonians, Egyptians, Persians began the physical training of young boys to brace them to be fierce battlers. The idea of superiority became so entrenched within ancient civilizations that the first Olympics were created to promote better body agility for being better warriors!

Romans and Greeks later started adding a tincture of philosophical ideas in this realm, believing in having a sound mind and body. This way, the energy was starting to be focused back on the intrinsic needs, called "art de vivre" back then.

Even though there were fluctuations in the European and American continent, Asia was ahead of all by starting early, thanks to the Chinese Kung-fu.

From the 5th to 15th century, the aspect of the body grew morose and folks all around the world started to view the afterlife as the ultimate success. Education condemned physical characters, and for money, the landlords exploited the physical traits of the labor. However, this period preceded the advent of biology, which also meant a change in lens towards the exterior traits. This period also included the legendary evolutionists, including Charles Darwin, who formulated the theory of the survival of the fittest in terms of reproductive fitness.

Fast-forwarding to the 20th century, European nations again turned to use physical education for having the best army. Similar situations were also seen in the U.S, however slightly later, since the U.S wasn't acutely vulnerable to foreign threats.

Gymnastics and Calisthenics stepped in, followed by the construction of gyms, all of them directed towards one primary goal: Military Preparedness.

But this era was peculiar in its own way as it also witnessed the birth of "Fitness" Market. Individuals like Edmond Desbonnet made physical fitness trendy through his fitness journal publications and by starting a chain of exercise clubs. Similar trends were observed in rest of the word and this was the birth of fitness in its own terms rather than for any other secondary goal. There were competitions, upsurge in the creation of unique equipment, and growth of other industries like that of supplements, DVDs, books, tech-based fitness, etc where each one competed to produce the fastest and the simplest fitness methods as possible.

While there was the advent of the new machinery on one end of dichotomy, the other end was covered in the science behind each Principle, studying and collecting the data in laboratories.

The current phase of the world is not astonishing. The keywords like fitness and physical activity now seem to be obsolete, yet the curve of sedentarism doesn't seem to be flattening. Even those who do remain in shape have some superficial purposes as the main goal rather than general well-being. The exercise equipment has been pervasive to such an extent that once the access is declined, the "fitness goals" are also diluted. The bodily movements are perceived more like a chore than an enjoyment, and the statistics reinforce it!

According to WHO, lack of physical activity is the fourth leading cause of global mortality, accounting for annually 2 million deaths. 35% of the Indians alone are not active, and according to WHO, there has been no deviation in these numbers since 2001.The number of cases of cardiovascular disease, diabetes, obesity, high blood pressure, and osteoporosis has never been higher.

Hence in this realm, it becomes imperative to be able to have complete control over the body. The way we establish control, however, can have some inherent variations. Tracing from the evolutionary point of view, we've evolved to be able to be engaged in tasks as mundane as walking, balancing, carrying, as well as life-threatening tasks like that of sprinting, swimming, jumping.

So, modern workouts could also be divided into 2 categories: Aerobic and Anaerobic. Going beyond the cliched definition that aerobic training relies more on oxygen, there lie some fundamental differences in the nature of how they're performed and what results they yield. Aerobic workouts are more like endurance workouts that are of moderate intensity in nature, and that of anaerobic are the high-intensity bursts like sprints.

Chapter: 2

Types of Training

Exercise has its rosy effects, yet only too few have the audacity to get on the track without fail. But how do we ensure we're reaping the optimum benefits?

We shall now look into how we classify these trainings into two different groups, and nutritional requirements specific to each training. This should give us a better broader picture of the types of exercises and help us choose the one by our needs.

But before I try to distinguish between these two groups, I would like to put forth two principles: The overload principle and principle of reversibility. According to the overload principle, when we perform a single exercise, regardless of the type, our muscles respective to the area we focus on produce some stress response. When we continue to exercise over a long period of time, those respective muscles become adaptive to the stress, making the stress response less severe than before. It is necessary to build adaptations since it increases our capacity to work without much effort.

You might have observed one person who could barely workout for 10 minutes in the beginning, but after say, around a month, he would go on without break for say, 40 minutes. This phenomenon is referred to as muscle plasticity. This not only helps us exercise better but also leads to increased fat utilization and spare carbohydrates. Remember, muscle plasticity comes with adaptation, so it is necessary on our side to keep up with the exercise.

But after you have developed endurance one might be like "Oh, I have got the fitness level I wanted, why to worry about exercising at all now?" But here's the subtle truth: our muscles also follow the principle of reversibility, that is if we stop training, all the progress would go to the baseline levels as if we never exercised. We shall discuss the particular examples under each training section.

1. Endurance Training- In this training, for optimal adaptation for muscles, there are 4 factors that govern its adaption: Training Frequency, Intensity, Duration, and the Mode of activity. For endurance training, the training frequency should be ideally 3 to 5 times a week (if you can exercise only thrice a week, it is better to do so on the alternative days rather than in the continuity). The exercise intensity should be moderate, which is 50 to 85% of your heart reserve, to be precise. Although you may remember these numbers while you workout, the only thing you need to keep in mind is that you need focus moderate exhaustion per cycle to be on the path of endurance training.

Taking from my perspective, when I started exercising, I started with a low to moderate-intensity exercise and gradually increased my intensity over the period of days I exercised. Although I did increase my intensity, I gradually morphed my endurance workouts into strength training. This way, I was getting adapted to the endurance workout without straining my muscles too much.

The duration of this type of exercise should be at least 20 minutes. And again, as we develop adaptation, one must try to increase the duration of the exercise up to a certain limit. For example, initially, when I started rope skipping, I could barely do it for say, a minute or so. But if you ask me today, I could go well over 25 minutes, though I avoid over-exhaustion.

The last variable is the mode of activity. The exercise we follow must involve a muscle group that can be maintained over time.

As I discussed earlier, one classic research on the principle of reversibility of endurance training includes previously sedentary individuals who underwent endurance training. The study measured various measures including their maximum oxygen uptake, and other variables which as predicted increased after training. But, when individuals were not engaged in any workout,they re-measured all the parameters. It was noticed that all the parameters went back to baseline.

Hence it becomes imperative for us to maintain the regularity of the exercise.

Since the 2 different types of exercises vary in the procedure and in results, it must not be a surprise that each of the training types has different nutritional requirements. I will bring 3 main factors of nutritional requirements into your notice: How much to eat, what to eat, and finally when to eat.

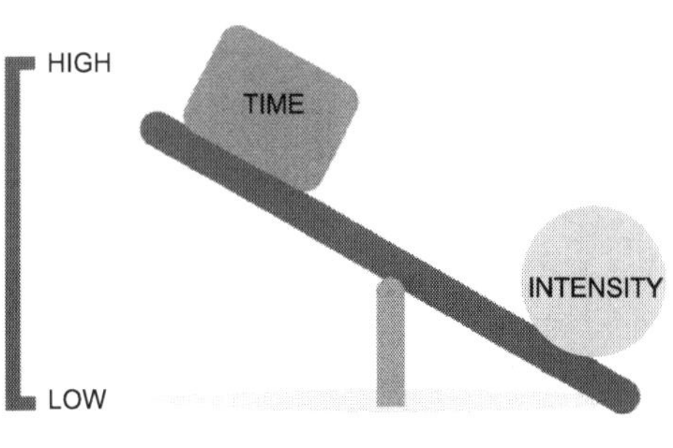

The endurance athletes must maintain their energy balance that is total energy intake must equal out the energy used. Negative energy balance (intake < expenditure) leads to weight loss, and positive energy balance (intake>expenditure) leads to the accumulation of fat in the body.

People following endurance training do not wish to carry extra fat on their body and hence, if they are overweight, they maintain a negative energy balance for some time. But, for the best results, maintaining an energy balance (neither positive nor negative) works out the best to enhance the performance since prolonged negative energy balance can lead to chronic fatigue.

Lets' come to our next factor that is "what to eat". The main goal for endurance training is preserving carbohydrate stores and using fat stores. So, it must not be astonishing if I tell you that for endurance athletes, carbohydrates must be the majority macronutrient in their diet (50-60% of the calories consumed). A study was conducted to compare the effects of a carbohydrate diet percentage on performance.It was found that their levels were higher by the 40% carb diet and hence, provides evidence of how important it was for them to maintain a high-carb diet.

Moving on to the 3rd factor, which is "when to eat"; approximately, it takes around 24 hours to replenish the drained glucose stores after a single bout of exercise. For optimum replenishment, food should be consumed within a 1-2 hour window post-exercise. The reason behind this lies in increased insulin sensitivity in the post-exercise period. As we went over in the endocrine system that insulin promotes the uptake of glucose by muscles, feeding glucose in this period would enhance the ability of our muscles to take in more glucose. Regarding the pre-training food timings, food should be consumed 2 to 3 hours prior to exercise and should be around 300-500 calories. This ensures that the majority of the blood flow goes to the working muscles and not the digestive system. Also, as we know that during the post-meal period, insulin levels are high, promoting glucose uptake by the muscles. Eating just before exercise will promote glucose uptake by all muscles, thereby reducing the glucose availability for the muscles doing the actual work.

Here's a **secret trick** through which you can boost your performance for the big competition day by increasing the glucose uptake by muscles just by altering the pre-exercise diet. Here's how it goes:

Perform strenuous exercise for about 7 days before the big competition day.

For the first 3 days, have an intake of a low-carb and high-fat and protein diet keeping the muscle glucose levels low.

For the last 3 days, switch to a high in carb diet.

In this method, initially, we are starving our muscles by keeping them deprived of precious glucose. As expected, as soon as we incorporate the glucose back in our diet, our muscles consume a lot excessive amount of glucose than do normally do (just like me, when I get home from school and gobble up my lunch, when I forget to carry one). This classic regimen was known to have some side effects on mood, so there's a modified regimen as well. In this, they reduce the intensity of exercise as compared to the classic regimen 7 days before the competition, and eat 70% of the carb diet days before the event as opposed to just 3 days. This method is more effective than the last one.

Finally, another important aspect I would like to emphasize on is the usage of performance enhancement drugs. One of the most common techniques used in the past by the athletes is the "Blood doping". In cases in which maximum oxygen consumption is required, blood doping can help increasing oxygen intake and therefore, enhance the performance. This involves the fusion of the athlete's own blood cells (classic blood doping), thus increasing the number of oxygen carriers.

OXYGEN CARRIERS WITH OXYGEN INSIDE THEM.

Another easier method for blood doping that athletes do is taking injections of erythropoietin, a hormone produced by the kidney that stimulates the RBC production in the bone marrow. However, this method involves a lot of risks as each body reacts differently to the injection of the hormone.

However, another common performance enhancer which most of us take is the sweet morning coffee. It is not actually coffee doing the work, but it is actually the caffeine in it which makes the difference. Although caffeine can enable you to pull an all-nighter to finish your final project, regular users can develop resistance and hence would require a higher dose each time they take caffeine. Caffeine in itself has other detrimental effects. In general, though performance enhancers can be tempting, staying away from them is the best way possible in order to get the maximum benefits from the exercise.

2. **Strength Training**- The principle of overloading also applies to strength training as well. So, let's look into the factor that helps in the optimizing of strength training. These factors are: Training Frequency, Intensity, number of repetition cycle(REP cycle), and the number of sets per session.

The main goal for this training is doing a low number of REP cycles but focusing on maximum intensity per REP cycle. That means the number of times you repeat an exercise should be low and whenever you do exercise, it should be of the maximum intensity.

When we do strength-training exercises, there is initially improvement in the neural adaptations which include better muscle coordination, and motor skills. This

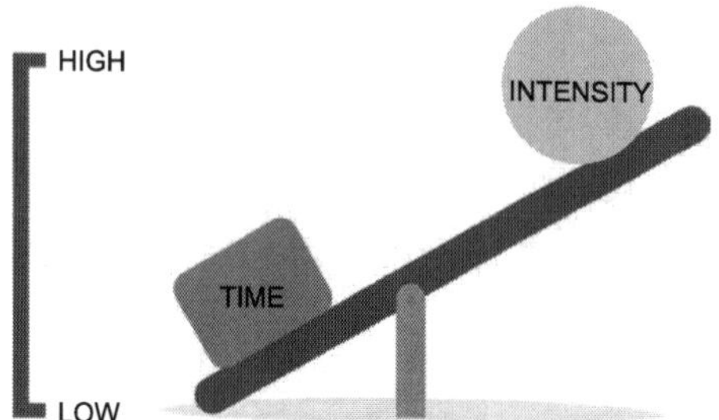

is followed then by increased muscle hypertrophy which results in the building up of the plateau by increased muscle cross-sectional area. In this case too, muscles are plastic; that is by over-chronic training, they grow bigger and stronger. But remember, the principle of reversibility is applicable over here as well. Hence dotn stop exercising!

Also, it has long been known that men are better at strength training than women. But why?

Typically, for equal muscle mass in both women and men, both of them generate an equal amount of force, hence there is no difference observed on the gender basis, once both men and women have undergone strength training. But what about the time during training? It turns out, in the neural adaptations, both men and women have an equal increase in strength. Hence during early training sessions, there is no difference over here as well.

Although during later stages of training, it is being noticed that men have a greater capacity to increase muscle mass which implies more muscle hypertrophy than women. Hence, women have to work relatively longer to get some muscle mass as men.

Nutritional requirements for strength training are pretty different from that of endurance training. These requirements can also be broken into 3 factors as in the endurance training. Since strength training mainly focuses on increasing the muscle mass, it is therefore to increase the rate of muscle protein breakdown. This can be done by increasing the amount of protein intake in our diet coupled with high-intensity exercise as I discussed earlier. This answers what to eat. Ideally, the strength trainers usually double the recommended protein making it closer to the 1.6 grams of protein per kilo body weight each day.

Considering when to eat, since protein synthesis increases in the post-exercise period, consumption of protein in the first hour of the post-exercise period can help us reach optimum level of protein.

A research was conducted which noted the increase in protein synthesis after the workout session, i.e. when combined with protein intake, it was found it further increased the synthesis rate by 30%!

In strength training as well, it is important for us to avoid the positive energy balance(more intake than calories burned), since it can result in various diseases later in life including obesity.

As in the case of endurance training, strength training also involves usage of performance enhancers which are also referred to as ergogenic aids. The extreme competitiveness in sports led to increased use of these drugs and hence, they were banned. Some of the methods employed included stacking, pyramiding, intaking growth hormone, etc. However, the benefits always come with some bitterness. In this case, those who employed these methods experienced various disorders and diseases like brain and liver cancer, heart and kidney disease, and whatnot. I cannot state this statement without more emphasis that taking those drugs has more downs than ups.

Chapter: 3

Body's Reaction to Exercise

We don't feel the same when we're working out versus, say, when learning a new concept. This is due to the fact that our body's homeostasis is disrupted in the former case. This disruption isn't a negative impact; rather it produces a change in the way macromolecules are consumed in our body.

ATPs (Adenosine Triphosphate) are like the energy bills that are paid for our workouts.

But the source of these ATPs is the Carbs which are constantly broken down as we further progress in our exercise. The issue is that glucose is sparse in our bodies and once it goes below the baseline levels, the fatigue sets in. However, out of carbs, proteins and fats, why do we heavily rely on those carbs for energy?

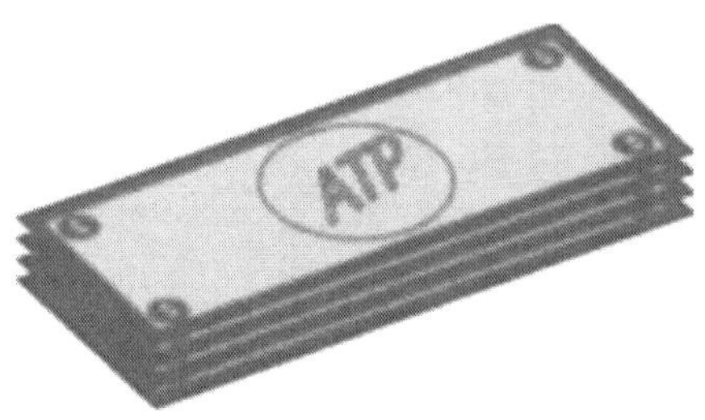

The dynamics of exercise somewhat influence the preferred source of energy. Fats require significant oxygen for it to break down. However, anaerobic workouts fail to fulfill this criterion. Still, even in these cases, fats can assist to provide energy in the early stages of the workout. Another reasons fat are not preferred source of transaction is because it take 6 hours for this transaction to be successful.

Proteins are more like the building blocks of the body, being in used up enzymes, and many other sources. So, they are more like assistants of glucose than being the primary source.

Some of the readers might question the motive behind knowing the source of energy derivation since the ultimate motive is weight loss; the chunk of skin fold deposited around your belly is the fat which you'd want to prune away. The energy source could make a difference because when one's dependent on glucose, we reach the stage of fatigue much earlier, because of the lack of glucose availability to support prolonged workouts.

CARBOHYDRATE SPARING

It may sound ironic to hear about sparing carbs, even after over-vilifying them in the diet chapter. However, to get in shape, the fats are something to be weeded out.

As I mentioned above, fats need a significant amount of oxygen to be generous in burning. This directs us towards adding aerobic exercises to our workouts along with prolonged, intermediate-intensity workouts. By following endurance training, our ability to use glucose also significantly increases.

This is not to say that ruling out anaerobic exercises would do good to you. Studies suggest that having mixed exercise intensities have shown optimum benefits in more or less, every parameter involved. Instead, occasionally following **carbohydrate loading** (intaking carbs before workouts) could make our exercise sustainable.

Personally, I am a big fan of high intensity/anaerobic workouts. However, I also do add the middle intensities in the nicks and on the days, when I feel like having a slight novelty.

The reason we're keeping protein out of the picture is that studies have shown that after workouts, there's an upsurge in the protein synthesis which assists in the growth and general building of our body, and not in providing energy to sustain a workout.

Chapter: 4

System's Reaction to Exercise

Learning about the metabolism of the macros was crucial to know what kind of exercises one must follow for optimum benefits, but exploring what exactly happens in our different body systems can also help us bust some common myths regarding exercising.

First in line is the **Muscular System**. This is something that we intuitively focus on when we first hear about exercise. While working out, our muscles undergo contractions to help us move. But which muscles are active depends on the type of exercise we're involved in.

There are 2 types of muscles: Type 1 and 2. During the moderate or aerobic exercise, type 1 muscles are used. These muscle fibers follow the aerobic pathway and thus help us last longer during exercising. They rely mainly on fat storage for the derivation of the energy.

But just like we switch our metabolism from that of fat to glucose when switching from aerobic to anaerobic workouts, even our muscles have a switch of their own– switch from type 1 to type 2 muscles.

Just as the situation demands, type 2 muscles meet all requirements: provide more power. But, it is for a short term. These muscle fibers rely on carbohydrate stores and after a certain time, one feels easily exhausted due to limited carbohydrate reserves.

An average individual relies 50% on type 1 muscle fibers and 50% on type 2. But, one can alter these dependency rates by changing the way we exercise, say, by endurance training. So, an endurance athlete will have more of type 1 and the sprinters will have more of type 2.

Through endurance training, one can increase the reliability of type 1 muscle fibers and burn more fats leading to weight loss.

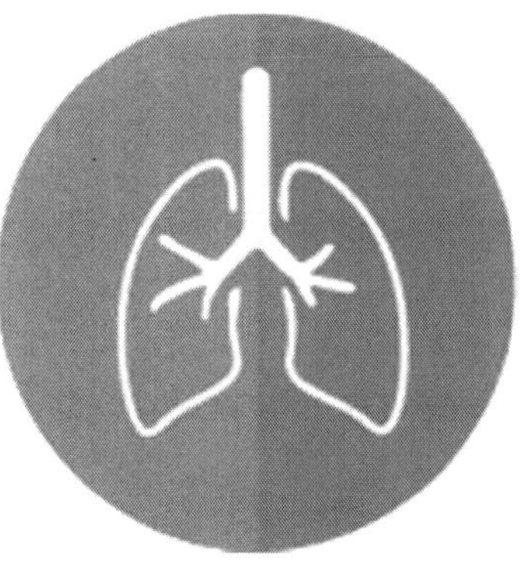

Let's now explore how our **respiratory system** reacts to the exercise. When we exercise, our respiratory system ensures that we are taking in a sufficient amount of oxygen,an essential component for energy production. The increase in oxygen intake is due to the increase in the ventilation rate. This increase not only provides us with more oxygen but also breaks the substances that causes muscle cramps.

Exercising also leads to the accumulation of carbon dioxide in the body. The respiratory system also ensures that the accumulated carbon dioxide doesn't stay for long and is removed from our body.

We all must have heard this good old saying: "Always exercise with fans and ACs turned off!" It's time to debunk the truth. One can compare sweating to a natural fan embedded in the body.

When it's turned on, it prevents your body to enter the overheated state. If we add an external cooler to the job as well, naturally you'd sweat less. But does less sweating have a correlation with less weight loss?

The answer is plain No. Exercise productivity is not impacted by the amount you sweating. If it were, then just sitting in the sun could do the job well.

Since we have looked into how this system adjusts to exercise, let's now briefly go over the implications of these adjustments.

Most of us most have seen athletes wearing nasal strips which are known for long to improve their performance by decreasing nasal airway resistance. If you haven't seen one, refer to the picture below.

A player with Nasal Strips on his nose.

But do these strips actually contribute to their better performance? Speaking scientifically, nasal stripes do not act as enhancers. Our lungs, during exercise, have a tremendous capacity to increase the ventilation hence is not considered as the limiting factor in the performance. Thus, even though nasal strips slightly reduce air resistance, they do not boost the athlete's performance. Yet, it is believed it has an indirect connection, psychologically, which actually helps the player to perform better than usual. This is called the placebo effect.

The last condition I would like to bring up here is "exercised induced asthma". As the name says, some of its main symptoms are shown in individuals running out of breath, coughing, having difficulty in breathing, etc. This is mainly due to the cold air and a high level of air pollution. Individuals who observe such symptoms must take special care during exercising outdoors.

After respiratory comes the **endocrine system**. This also has far-reaching applications from impacting body system priorities to even curing diabetes.

Each of its glands secretes hormones that are crucial for our body. Whenever we eat something, our blood glucose levels shoot up. To balance this, the pancreas secretes a hormone called insulin which encourages the muscles to take up glucose and thus replenish their stores. But when we exercise, the insulin secretion reduces. You might wonder, why would the insulin secretion decrease if it's aiding in the glucose absorption by our muscles?

Well, as we exercise, we also observe an increase in the blood flow to the working muscles. Due to this increase in flow, those muscles actually end up getting a boost in the insulin and hence, get more glucose to obtain sufficient energy. This also helps cut down the glucose intake by other systems which don't aid in exercising, in order to maximize the supply for the active muscles.

Besides this, exercising also increases insulin sensitivity. Improving insulin sensitivity is crucial because 90-95% of all diabetic patients have type 2 diabetes, which is primarily caused by insulin resistance.

Another gland I'd bring up is the pituitary gland, the orchestra conductor of all the other glands. Under this, growth hormone is something that gets a lot of attention because of its charismatic effects of bringing about the growth in our body.

While we exercise, the growth hormone secretion, like other non-essential tasks, is suppressed. But after a workout, studies have shown that their levels remain elevated for about an hour, hence supporting growth. For the most optimum results in growth, **endurance exercise** should be the go-to.

The next system is the **Cardiovascular System.** While exercising, it's a common observation that our heart pounds faster than usual. But what could this have an implication as?

Regular exercising causes changes in our body to increase the blood flow towards the muscles which need oxygen and energy, the most. This increase in blood flow not only aids our working muscles but also cleanses our blood vessels and saves us from heart attacks!

Last but not least is the Immune System. Immunity is especially a hot topic nowadays during COVID, so this must be something worthwhile to unravel.

The truth is that while exercising, you become more susceptible to the floating micro-organisms around you! As baffling as it sounds, this is the truth. Also, as I had told earlier that exercising has an impact on releasing of hormones, these hormones actually suppress our immune system. To prove this, research was conducted which included one group of participants who recently completed a big marathon like Tour de France, and the other group which included people who did not complete the marathon but had similar fitness when compared to the athletes. The results showed that even weeks later, marathon participants were 2 to 5 times more likely to get infected as compared to the non-participants.

This helps us conclude to avoid working out when one's under the weather. The thumb rule is to avoid any exertion and take as much rest as you can. If you have symptoms of ailments below the neck, like pain in the stomach, muscle ache, fever, etc, then avoid exertion at all costs. If the symptoms are above the neck, like headache, light exercising can be alight unless you don't strain yourself or feel uncomfortable. Again, if you are uncomfortable, it would be best advised to stop working out and take as much rest.

The good news is that long-term exercising, in fact, boosts our immunity. It has been even shown that obesity significantly increases the chances of severe symptoms of COVID 19.

Even after finding the charismatic impact of exercise on our body, one corner still remains unanswered: The Brain.

Chapter: 5

The Growth

Our brain is the most fascinating machine in our universe. From processing the raw electric signals it receives from our eyes to sending an output of a vibrant new world, to even aiding in breakthroughs that shape our lives; without it, life wouldn't have its syllables!

Hence, it's imperative for us to keep this wonder in its most puerile state, and also enhance it to the next levels. And exercise serves to be a perfect elevator for this.

Exercise stimulates many activities throughout the body; its aura isn't restricted from the brain, either. Exercise makes our brain secrete hormones like serotonin and epinephrine, which reduce depression, regulate anxiety, maintain bone health, and also heal wounds!

But there still remains yet another advantage that has made me fell in love with exercise, over and over and again. This is like a genie's potion for the young people out there that can help them solve all their stresses, complaints, and desires.

The answer is that exercise even has the potential to boost the memory power of our brain! This is done by growing the intricacies of the existing connections in the brain, through a protein called Brain Derived Neurotrophic Factor or BDNF.

Like a soil fertilizer catalyzes the growth of a plant, so does the BDNF for our brain. This is what helps in boosting our long term memory formation and it even acts as an anti-depressant.

NEURONS, LIKE THIS TREE, GROWING WHEN SPRINKLED WITH BDNF

If you sprinkle BDNF on the neurons on a Petri dish, you would notice that the neurons grow and become denser. In fact, BDNF is called master molecule and is also referred to as "Miracle Gro for the brain" by a Harvard neuropsychiatrist, John J. Ratey, for the miraculous functions it performs.

Another author and "Evolutionary fitness expert", Eva De Vany agrees with Dr. Ratey and explains why BDNF is so advantageous in improving our performance, intelligence, and longevity- "When BDNF is released, new connections form in the brain as the BDNF attracts new dendrites from nerve cells to connect to other cells or their synapses. As the brain cells "fire together", they "wire together". Wiring new networks together helps memory formation and consolidation. A neural network is a thought, a memory, or a new skill. This "fast" form of learning is essential in emergency situations where fight or flight may be the only means of coping. Evolution would seem to require that fast learning takes precedence in fight or flight situations, and the release of BDNF and stress hormones during such episodes almost assures that the event is registered as salient and important."

This is such a crucial protein that its absence paves the way for diseases like Alzheimer's Disease, and Eating disorders and depression.

Chapter: 6

Boosting BDNF

With so many benefits this one protein has, it feels like we should try to have more of it! Indeed, students want to improve their grades, and so, improving the BDNF levels might be one of the best ways possible. But is it just the exercise that we all need for pumping up the BDNF productions? Before any of you starts setting your rigorous exercise plans, I would like to say simply, that answer is “NO”! Of course, exercise is crucial for BDNF production, but there are some more ways as well to boost up the BDNF production.

Methods to improve the BDNF are:-

1. **Low Sugar Intake**- Diets high in sugar levels reduce BDNF production. This diet includes carbonated drinks, processed foods, and refined sugary products. Sticking to natural food is the best way possible for optimal brain functioning.

A DEMONSTRATION OF HOW YOUR NEW ACTIONS SHOULD AFFECT CARBS: DESPERATE FOR YOU TO EAT THEM.

2. **Intermittent Fasting-** Intermittent fasting has also shown to contribute towards the increase in the BDNF production rate. As we have already discussed in the diet section, intermittent fasting helps in decreasing insulin levels, impacting positively on the expression of genes related to longevity and disease protection.

3. **Sprints and Exercise-** As we have already discussed that exercise stimulates our brain to produce BDNF, then what's so special about the sprint workouts?

A German study discovered that sprints resulted in 20% better learning when compared to low-intensity aerobic exercises. The subject's vocabulary also increased in both the short term and the long term sprints. Sprinting not only increased the levels of BDNF, but also other hormones like dopamine (which gives short term memory boosts), epinephrine, and norepinephrine.

These drastic improvements were noticed with only 2 sprint workouts. For example, sprinting for 3 minutes and taking a 2-minute break, and again sprinting for 3 minutes– after just this much physical activity, you can enjoy as much as a 20% increased learning ability!

4. **High-Intensity Resistance Training (HIRT)-** High-Intensity Resistance Training is nothing but intense periods of resistance training (done with a lot of effort and concentration) with some recovery periods between the exercises. This type of exercise gets your heart racing since the recovery periods are kept short, which leads to massive calorie burn along with muscle stimulations.

This training is short which does not lead to boredom, and burns more calories in less amount of time. This happens in 2 ways:

A. DURING EXERCISE- Since this training already involves high-intensity exercises; this burns more than normal calories.

B. POST EXERCISE- This period is called EPOC which stands for Excess post exercise oxygen consumption. This is a period when your body starts restoring its normal functions. Considering the intensive nature of HIIT, these periods after HIIT tend to be longer and hence contribute more, around 6-15% extra calorie burn.

Also, for those of you who love the intense but short workouts, this might be a perfect match for you.

The best thing about these exercises that you don't need to find a partner for it or even go to a gym! It does not require any equipment, so it can be done at home as well.

But, let's say your exercise is something that cannot be assessed with the number of times you do, like in running. So in these cases, make sure you keep your exercise to recovery ratio as 1:1. For example, running vigorously for 3 minutes, and then following it by a 3-minute low-intensity workout like a walk. Another type of program under the HIIT is called "spring interval training". In this, basically, you run for 30 seconds at the maximum speed that you can, followed by approx. 4 minute recovery time (low-intensity workout) and you do this task in multiple REPs.

As we have discussed the effects of exercise on the brain earlier, and since HIRT is also an exercise, it obviously becomes a contributor to the BDNF creation.

Resistance training, in general, has always been a preference over moderate training. This is because, in a study consisting of subjects aged 65 to 75, the participants were divided into 2 groups: one underwent Resistance training and the other underwent moderate training. The results showed that the resistance training group showed improvement in verbal and spatial memory.

And in another study consisting of women aged 65-75, who had never performed resistance training before, participants were split into 2 groups again: one exercised for around 60 minutes with sets of 8 reps, and the other did balanced exercises. The first group was further classified into 2 parts: one which did resistance training once a week, and the other which did twice a week. After comparison of this group to the other group which did balanced exercises for 60 minutes, it was found that resistance training group showed significant improvements in executive functions (like planning, decision making, and multi-tasking) for both, once a week and twice a week participants.

These studies depict how much of importance resistance training carries as compared to other exercises.

5. **Enriched Social Environment** - You might have not seen this coming, but studies have shown that an enriched social environment leads to an increase in neurotrophic activity. This means that there must be more of BDNF. We, humans, are designed to be working in groups rather than working alone.

An Italian study found that children who grow up in a socially rich environment have higher neurotrophic levels and reflect better social skills later in life.

A similar study found that enriching social surroundings also led to decreased levels of depression and anxiety later in life, possibly due to increased neurotrophic activity.

This all also makes sense from the fact that prisoners are left alone in an isolated room which is considered as a severe punishment!

6. **Sunlight (Vitamin D)**- Netherlands' scientists found that levels of BDNF changed with the changing season. This confirmed that higher is the amount of sunlight, more is the BDNF level.

This may also help to link illnesses to seasonal changes. Also, why do we find a city covered in snow, depressing (say, Kashmir) and another city of the same country which does not receive snow, rejuvenating (say, Mumbai)? Well, we had discussed that lack of BDNF levels leads to a number of problems, one of which is depression and anxiety. So, this might be a plausible answer to the question.

7. **Chewing more food** - In a normal case, it is not the BDNF that aids in the learning process; it is that protein which BDNF increases the level of, which, in turn, aids in improving memory retention. So in normal cases, more is the BDNF, more is that downstream protein.

But in a research conducted on mice, in which the experimental group was given more of a liquid diet and the control group ate the normal chewing food, the results showed that although the BDNF increased, the downstream protein actually decreased in case of the liquid diet. Since the protein decreased, the BDNF boost didn't show any enhancement in learning.

Hence if you mostly have a liquid diet, chewing a gum would provide you the beneficiary results!

Chapter: 7

Roots of BDNF

BDNF is a charismatic protein– we all have our heads cleared up on this. But now, it's actually the time to unravel some of the hidden associations within our body, related to BDNF.

1. **BDNF and the Weight** - BDNF controls food intake through hippocampal signaling. Studies have experimented by injecting BDNF in rats and found that BDNF caused a decrease in the rat's body weight and suppressed their diet.

In humans, it is observed that people who are suffering from obesity, and type 2 diabetes tend to have a lower level of BDNF. In layman's terms, the less the BDNF is, the fatter is the person.

Lower BDNF is a symptom, or a factor of obesity, whereas higher BDNF levels help people to weigh less.

2. **BDNF and the Sleep**- In some of the studies, researchers have found that BDNF tends to ameliorate depression-like symptoms. It is also noticed that antidepressants contain chemicals that stimulate the production of BDNF, thus lowering depression. As the level of depression decreases, the duration of sleep tends to increase.

3. **BDNF and Well Being-** Since we know that the more the BDNF is, the better is the learning. This enables people to acquire more knowledge and hence makes them feel happier. It has also shown some correlation with decreased depression levels.

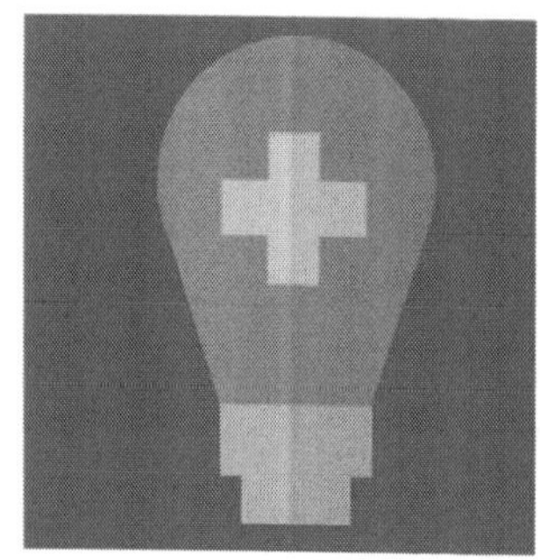

BDNF also has a link with heart diseases because of the fact that mice that are engineered to have BDNF-lacking hearts easily develop heart failure. Some studies have also observed that BDNF prevents the exhaustion of the pancreas in diabetic mice as it restores the insulin-secreting hormones in the pancreas.

It has also been observed that brain size shows a positive correlation, particularly amongst mammals, and BDNF may be the connecting link between the two. Dietary restrictions can increase the BDNF levels in the brain and thus make neurons more resistant to aging. Interestingly, BDNF can also increase insulin sensitivity, thus providing a mechanism for the brain to control its life span.

But since every pro has con to it, increased BDNF levels also lead to an increase in blood pressure. And what's more, excessive BDNF in the forebrain can hinder the memory consolidation, resulting in poor learning.

People with genetically lower BDNF production have lower blood pressure.

I hope this provides you with an insight that increasing BDNF is indeed essential but as the old man says "Too much of everything is bad", the same applies for BDNF as well.

Chapter: 8

Learning From Animals

So far, we have looked at what BDNF is, its effects on the brain, and the ways to naturally increase its production rate.

In order to examine to what degree learning is influenced by the exercise, a study was conducted placing mice in two cages, one with a running wheel which allowed them to exercise, and the other with a non-running wheel to prevent them from exercising. Since mice love running, they can run for hours and cover kilometers overnight.

Later, the two groups of mice were placed in a water maze, in which they had to learn to swim to a safer water level. When the runners were compared to the non-runners, the researchers found that runners learned faster when compared to the non-runners. The runners performed significantly better than the mice which were kept with toys and other colorful objects which are known to stimulate the brain growth.

This one experiment raises tons of more questions, like how much exercise is required for the stimulation? And does this exercise need to be done daily or occasionally?

In an experiment, rats were again divided into 2 groups; one group which had daily exercised on the running wheel, and the other which was exposed to running wheel on alternating days.

The experiment revealed that the group which had daily access to the running wheel showed a 174% rise of the BDNF than its original level!

In the case of the intermittent group, they had shown an increase of 160% of the original BDNF level, indicating the need to exercise regularly.

But what happens if we actually stopped exercising?

In a similar experiment, the wheels of both the mice groups (the daily runners, and intermittent runners) were locked, and then their BDNF levels were observed. It was found that there was a gradual decline in the levels, and it took about 14 days for daily runners, and 3 days for intermittent runners to completely reset the BDNF levels to the point from where there was no upsurge.

Later, they put the same group of mice, which stopped running, back to running. They found that if the animals began running, their BDNF levels soared again as if it never went down.

But how much gap can we afford to ensure that BDNF levels soar high again when we start back our exercise routine?

To answer this question, the researchers compared the mice group who took a week's break from running to the group which took a 2-week break. They found that the BDNF increased levels didn't show any significant differences.

These studies provide us greater insights and clear out many misconceptions. This proves that exercising definitely has a positive correlation with learning. Exercising regularly has shown higher benefits in learning (higher BDNF levels) than exercising intermittently. Also, if we don't exercise, our improvement goes back to its baseline level as if it never went up (goes down much faster in the case of intermittent exercising than that of regular exercising). So, we need to constantly exercise to enjoy its benefits in learning. And one of the greatest misconceptions among people is that if they don't exercise for a certain amount of time, the results they saw earlier become difficult to be noticeable and it becomes more difficult to restart, the longer we don't exercise. But, the studies have also proved that taking a pause may not be as detrimental as you think.

We have discussed quite a lot about BDNF, since there's just so much to talk about this special protein, that I can't help it.

Chapter: 9

Reviving Yoga

The word "Yoga" might not be new for most of us. In fact, it's so widespread that chances of not observing it in action are minuscule. But let's be honest here, it is thought to be an activity long associated with people who are aged, or who are looking for their peace of mind. We will discuss its misconceptions and other related facts later, but for now, let's try to understand what it really is.

In layman terms, it simply means taking the control of your body and assuring all the parts are synchronized; by being its own mechanic and not paying others to do so (especially, to medical professionals).

Yoga is performed in different versions like Hatha yoga, Raja yoga, Swara yoga, and many more. I will not go in-depth about its different versions since this is trivial for what my main purpose is.

In yoga, there are different asanas (postures), named as per their resemblance to objects or animals like tree, snake, eagle, plough, each of which targets different parts of our body. A pose is maintained for a couple of minutes, and involves deep breathing and inhaling and exhaling as we progress in an asana.

Yoga routines can vary anywhere from 20 minutes to an hour, but for school kids, 30 minutes are more than sufficient in a day. Yoga must be practiced regularly in order to see its benefits.

One question: is it any good?

Answer: Resounding yes!

1. **Decreases Stress Levels**- A study had been conducted which tested 24 women who considered themselves as emotionally unstable. Following a three-month yoga program, their stress levels were measured again and were found to be lower.

Another study with 131 participants who took part in a 10-week yoga program also showed a decrease in their stress and anxiety and depression levels.

Hence these studies prove that yoga helps to curb down the stress which can cause various diseases and disorders including fatigue and headaches.

2. **Relieves Anxiety**- Most of the people do yoga to control their anxiety levels. In a study consisting of 34 women diagnosed with anxiety disorder, the participants took part in yoga classes twice a week for 2 months. After 2 months, the levels of their anxiety were significantly lower and better than the control group.

In a different study, 64 women participants were selected who suffered from post-traumatic stress disorder (PTSD). PTSD is triggered by horrifying events, after either experiencing or witnessing them. This may include flashbacks, nightmares, and severe anxiety attacks; usually because of not being able to cope out of the situation and move on. After 10 weeks, 52% of the participants were not categorized as PTSD patients at all!

It's not exactly clear how yoga is able to do that, but yoga helps us to be in the present, and find peace of mind.

3. **Helps reduce inflammation**- Inflammation is basically

our immune response to eradicate the diseases from our body. But sometimes, our immune system may wrongly interpret this, and end up killing our own cells and lead to diseases like diabetes, heart disease, and even cancer.

In 2015, a study included 218 participants and was made to do moderate and vigorous exercises to induce stress. Then, the participants were further divided into 2 groups, one which practiced yoga and the other which didn't. By the end, the results showed that the yogis had lower inflammatory markers.

Another small study has shown that 12 weeks of yoga decreased the inflammatory markers in even cancer survivors who persistently felt fatigued.

4. **Improves Heart Health**- We all know the importance of the heart. From pumping blood to various organs, to passing on oxygen in the blood, Heart performs many tasks for our body. So, it is our duty to keep it in its best shape possible. And studies have shown that yoga does this job perfectly well. Some of the other benefits of yoga are quite intuitive too.

A study found that the people who aged 40 above and practiced yoga showed lower blood pressure levels than those who didn't. Higher blood pressure is one of the major causes of numerous heart problems, and lowering BP can be one of the effective ways to prevent those problems.

Studies also suggest that incorporating yoga in our lifestyle could also slow down the progression of possible heart disease. A study observed changes in 113 patients with heart disease by incorporating yoga in their routine along with some dietary changes and stress management.

It was seen that the patients saw a 23% decrease in their total cholesterol and a 26% reduction in their bad cholesterol. Although it is still unclear how much of the role yoga played in comparison with other factors like diet, it is clear that bringing yoga in the lifestyle is definitely worth it!

5. **Promotes Sleep Quality and Relieves Migraines**- Poor sleep quality is related to obesity, high blood pressure, and depression. A study done in 2005 observed 69 elderly patients who were given options to choose from yoga, taking some herbal preparation, or being in the control group. And undoubtedly, Yoga participants not only fell asleep faster but also had a better night's sleep.

Migraines are severe repeating headaches and has more than 150 million cases in India. Yoga also aids in reducing migraines. In a 2007 study, 72 patients were divided into either a yoga group or self-care therapy group for three months. Yoga practitioners experienced reduced headache intensity, frequency, and pain compared to others.

In order to see if yoga also benefits those who have been taking conventional treatments before, another study on 60 patients was conducted by dividing them among those who did yoga and those who didn't, while both the groups still received conventional treatment. In this case as well, yogis seemed to outshine the other group.

6. **Improves Flexibility, Balance, and Strength**- One of the main motives of people in adding yoga is to increase their overall body flexibility and strength. Research also backs up this idea and proves it can optimize our performance by targeting specific postures.

A recent study looked at the effects of yoga on 26 college male athletes. It was seen that yoga had increased flexibility and balance relative to the non-yogis.

But does yoga increase the flexibility and strength of only the young ones, or does it even does so for the elderly? Another study answers this question. It included 66 elderly participants who either practiced yoga or calisthenics, a type of bodyweight exercise. After a year, the yoga practitioners had around 4 times the flexibly levels when compared to those who performed calisthenics.

Yoga also shows it magic by improving our body strength, endurance, and weight loss.

6. **Promotes eating healthy and mindfulness**- Many of us tend to multi-task and try to consume most out of some tasks which might appear trivial, or at least, it happened to me. For example, many often tend to try cramming for an upcoming test while eating, trying to make the best of the time. But what we don't realize is that we are not being mindful of what we eat.

Mindful eating, also called intuitive eating, is basically being in the moment while eating. It includes paying attention to the texture, color, and the smell of the food we eat and being aware of our thoughts while eating.

This way, we not only would be aware of what we are eating but also would not overeat. This helps to control blood sugar levels, increase weight loss, and improve disordered eating behavior.

A study included yoga in an eating disorder treatment program consisting of 54 patients. It was found that it reduced eating disorder symptoms.

This proved that yoga reduces the cravings of binge-eating, which in turn contributes to weight loss.

Thus, yoga can be an effective way to lose weight and can also enable us to remember what we ate during the day (which most of us don't) hence preventing overeating.

7. **Improves Breathing**- Yoga incorporates a number of breathing practices that include *pranayama*

But what do I actually mean by breathing? Does this mean just improving the breathing "in and out" procedure? No. It means increasing the breathing capacity of our lungs so that we don't go out of breath faster. In a study that consisted of 287 collegiate students who took 15 weeks of classes and were taught some yoga and breathing exercises; by the end of the 15th week, they had an increased breathing capacity. So, the next you find yourself out of breath after a short distance, you know what to do.

8. **Helps to Lose Weight**- After all the benefits we have discussed so far, this automatically becomes intuitive, so let's try to look into some of the studies done on this relation.

In 2013, a review supported by NCCIH reviewed 17 yoga-based programs and found that most of the participants had a moderate reduction in their weight. The programs which showed the best results included at least one of the following:-

A. Longer and more frequent yoga sessions

B. Longer program duration

C. Yoga-based dietary components

D. Practicing at Home

Another review in 2016 reviewed studies related to yoga and weight loss and found that yoga was related to lowering our BMI (BMI is Body Mass Index and is a tool for measuring our body fat relative to our height and weight).

There are other benefits as well which might not be that well known. For example, in a 2014 report which reviewed around 10 studies on yoga-based intervention and quitting smoking; in most instances, yoga helped to curb the urge to smoke.

You may ask that we have already seen it's a wide range of networking in our body, so it should also have some relation with preventing age-related brain loss? And you guessed that right!

Another study compared the grey matter of the participants found that there was a well-noticeable grey matter decline due to aging in the non-yogis. While in yogis, there were no such results. Also, it was also noticed that more the time a person practiced yoga, more was the volume of the brain, especially in the left brain hemisphere and hence it resulted in positive states. This study also analyzed different combinations of yogic practices and their effects on the brain. The results showed that a combination of asanas (postures) and meditation impacted the size of the hippocampus and parietal lobes (interprets sensory information) the most. It was also observed that the combination of meditation and breathing exercises contributed the most to the visual cortex (part of the brain which processes visual information) volume.

After reading its long benefit-list, one question might arise, how does yoga compare to other forms of exercise?

The answer is it depends on what form of yoga you are doing. If it involves just the relaxation exercise, then you are not going to build up muscles. However, some of the yoga forms like that of *ashtanga* can be comparable to the strenuous exercises.

Although speaking from a common-sense perspective, if the main goal is building up muscle or developing aerobic capacity, then the relaxation yoga poses wouldn't get your heart going up and thus might not be a better fit.

As we have discussed earlier that yoga increases our self-consciousness, it is found that those who practice yoga are likely to have better body awareness than those who do aerobic exercises.

Hence, practicing yoga for 15 to 30 minutes each day can do wonders. Even for a school going kid, it can be easily done at any point of the day. Personally, I would recommend doing it before going to school which can show positive effects in the academic areas as well. What it would only take is making time for those 15 minutes by either waking up a bit earlier or maybe cutting time from other activities to compensate for it. In case if you are not an early bird, doing it in the evening before the dinner can also be beneficial. Practicing and sticking to the routine even for a couple of days a week would be enough to see its magic come into play.

Chapter: 10
Exercise As Pill

So far, we have looked a lot into different body and brain responses to exercises, and various other responses produced by the exercise and whatnot. Most of you might be like "Mridul, I think you have covered everything, what else possibly a 30-minute experience could do?" Well, I think we all are skipping another crucial factor that exercise serves in our life: as a medicine. I think most of us are aware of the fact that exercise also has the medicinal effect in our life, but only a few of us know the specifics.

For starters, here are some facts: Those who spend hours sitting in front of the TV are at 61% greater risk of death as compared to those who watch TV less than an hour a day. Out of all the deaths, 20% of people die of having a sedentary lifestyle. The most common health problem across the world is obesity. Basically, all the males and females with a fat percentage higher than 25% and 35% respectively are considered obese.. It is also being noted that the total medical costs and lost work productivity due to increased absenteeism now costs greater than $200 billion annually.

Moving on from facts, it is being observed that mere exercise is the best possible treatment for type 2 diabetes.

1. It can also lower the chances of some of the common cancers

2. In old aged people, there is a loss of skeletal mass due to osteoporosis. Exercise helps in overcoming this by building endurance.

EXERCISE AS A PILL

A study was conducted to see whether having higher walking mile numbers provided any benefit. It was found that those who walked for 9+ miles a week had 21% lesser chances of mortality than those who walked for 3 or fewer miles a week. Another study tried to compare the mortality rate with the fitness level and observed that moving from the least fit group to the second least fit group resulted in a 50% decrease in the mortality rate.

Now, let's briefly look into some of the most common and lethal diseases and how exercise elevates the situation:

EXERCISE AND THE HEART DISEASE

While there can be many different types of heart diseases, I shall specifically focus on coronary heart disease here since it is the most common reason for death around the world. To start with, the major cause of this is atherosclerosis, which is basically the disease of arteries. Initially, there is the deposition of fats and cholesterol in the oxygen-carrying arteries. Gradually, the fat builds up in the arteries leading to partial or complete blockage causing chest pains and heart attacks.

Shown above is the image depicting the formation of plaque in our arteries leading to blockage. The yellowish substance

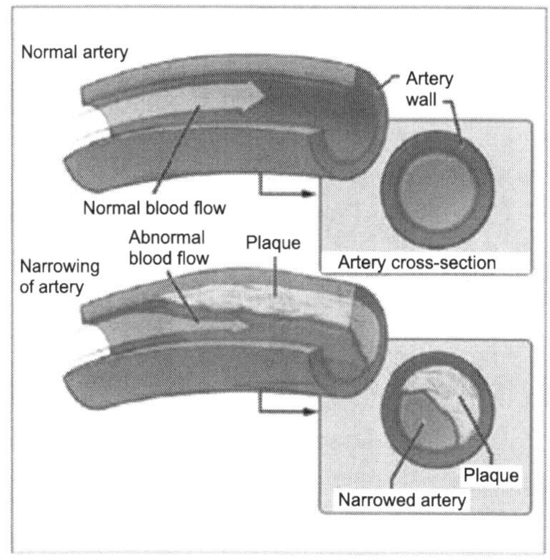

building up is fats. The major risk factors leading to this situation are obesity, physical inactivity, hypertension, high blood and lipid levels in the body, and type 2 diabetes. Let's see if exercise can contribute to lower the impact of all those factors.

Inactivity- Exercise involves body movement; hence physical inactivity is the first thing to be in the rules.

High lipid levels- There are basically 2 types of lipids in our body: The high density and the low-density ones. The High-Density Lipids (HDL) is considered good cholesterol while the Low-Density Lipids (LDL) are considered the harmful ones that deposit on the arteries forming plaques. Exercise has shown to impact these levels. While there may not be an overall change in the cholesterol level, exercise increases the HDL and decreases the LDL thereby eliminating this factor as well.

Hypertension- Physical activity has shown to be effective in reducing those numbers as efficiently as medications but also without any side effects. A study conducted in previously hypertension patients found that 9 months of aerobic exercise intervention ameliorated their conditions; however, the training effect was also reversed when detained for a month.

Diabetes- I shall discuss diabetes as a disease of its own.

Hence, we clearly can see that coronary heart disease can be avoided or reversed with the proper intervention of physical activity.

EXERCISE AND DIABETES

Out of all diabetic cases, 90-95% of cases are type 2 diabetes and I have already said earlier that exercise is the best remedy for this diabetes. Let's understand how. Type 2 diabetes is also referred to as non-insulin-dependent diabetes which is primarily caused by the development of insulin resistance. Some of the common symptoms include increased thirst, fatigue, frequent urination.

But why is diabetes such a big deal? Why do we need to come out of it in the first place? Well, diabetes is like a root which leads to countless various problems like causing blindness, kidney diseases, coronary heart diseases and whatnot.

Before going back to the question of how exercise lowers diabetic effect, let's recall insulin resistance I went over in the diet section. Basically, when our body stops responding to the cries of insulin which helps prevent diabetes, it arises a state called insulin resistance. But how do we know if one is suffering from insulin resistance or not? To know that, there are various tests out in the market, one of which is the oral glucose test. This always involves the consumption of a glucose drink after overnight fasting and monitoring the rate at which the individual's body clears the glucose from the blood. Insulin resistant individual takes longer to clear glucose. Hence exercise can improve this condition in 2 ways:

A. Decreasing the blood glucose levels.

B. Increasing insulin sensitivity

As we discussed earlier, during exercise, our working muscles take more and more glucose from blood thereby lowering the markers.

Regarding the second way, studies have shown that both endurance and strength training exercises help in improving insulin sensitivity proving that Type 2 diabetes is inversely related to the frequency of exercise. Fun fact: strength training does this job better since it relies primarily on blood glucose levels.

EXERCISE AND HEALTHY AGING

This might be the topic most of the readers are interested in. Who doesn't want to delay aging in this world anyway? But looking practically, physiological delay in aging isn't possible yet, but through exercise, one can prevent some other losses that come with it such as decreased bone weight, muscle mass, maximum oxygen capacity, stamina and whatnot, which would enable us to be independent and be away from these wheelchairs. For example, the pressure exerted on our bones by regular workouts increase the calcium deposition in our muscles and hence prevents osteoporosis, a common disease in the elderly people. People in their 90s can also reap the benefits of exercise. Although it's found that those who were active in both their early and their later years reaped the most benefit; individuals, who earlier were sedentary, after starting regular exercise, can decrease their mortality rate by 50%. Hence, it's never too late to get back in those sweaty pants!

WEIGHT LOSS

The solution to all the problems discussed above is by exercising and "losing weight". But losing weight is not that simple. Practically, everyone I met so far who knew about my weight loss journey was keen to know the "hack" to it. But here's a pro tip: there's in fact no single plan that guarantees success. But before I go into specifics about the different plans, I want to include the big idea of how weight loss actually occurs.

An individual tends to gain weight when he's taking more calories than being burned, which is also called a positive energy balance. So technically, in order to lose weight one has to be in negative energy balance i.e. burn more than consume. So my math says cutting down the food we eat should be more than enough for shedding that pile of junk right? Wrong! That stubborn layer around us isn't that easy to get rid of. Alone dieting can do some initial work but that would be due to the loss of water and not the fat burn. 90-95% of the individuals regain the weight they lost from solely dieting. To even make matters worse, weight loss by dieting also leads to loss of protein from our skeletal muscle. But how does the loss of skeletal muscle mass impact us? Well, skeletal muscles contribute to the resting metabolic rate in sedentary people which accounts for around 75% of the total calorie burn, hence making it an important aspect of our life. Those who exercise have a resting metabolic rate account for a relatively lower percentage that is 60%.

But, another question: So can exercise alone be the turning point in our life? It is being concluded that total energy expenditure has an inverse relation with obesity i.e. higher the energy spent -lower the obesity. But we also know that we need a negative energy balance for weight loss. In reality, mere exercise is not enough to produce that negative balance and hence, individuals who are solely relying on exercise quit in a month if they don't see the scale point changing.

So what exactly is a better plan?? Without a doubt, the middle path is the best path. Combining the 2 factors produces the best results. For instance: if an individual cuts down his calorie intake by 500 calories a day, and also increases his energy spent by 500 calories, he can lose 2-3 pounds a week. What's more- after a week, the majority of weight loss is by loss in fat and there is no decrement in their resting metabolic rate.

There's also a misconception amongst individuals that the medicinal benefits of the exercise can only be achieved by losing weight. But, let me be clear- even if the obese and overweight individuals don't see a significant change in the weighing scale does not mean they are not receiving other benefits. They are still having an edge of others by reducing their chances of lethal diseases like heart disease, cancers, etc.

So, next time you find yourself in the debate between whether or not you should go for that run…JUST DO IT.

Takeaways

1. There are mainly 2 types of exercises: aerobic and anaerobic, each of them having its own perks.
2. Endurance training focuses on length more than intensity. Hence it's important to stretch our duration as much as possible.
3. Meals should be consumed 2-3 hours before the workouts or else the energy would be distributed amongst all other muscles, reducing the energy available for our working muscles.
4. Limit the intake of energy drinks or coffee in general which provide short term energy boosts, as they can cause to develop resistance hence, making us have a more intake of them. Save those coffee shots only for the big days to get maximum benefit.
5. Main focus of strength training is to have lower repetitions but each cycle should be of high intensity, opposite of endurance training.
6. Strength training results in building better muscle mass and brain coordination.
7. For maximum benefits, consume a protein rich diet. Taking protein within an hour of the workout can do wonders.
8. Performance enhancers are used by some athletes to gain a short term performance boost. But that sweet little boost does bring bitterness with it.
9. Our body loves Carbs, but has a lesser preference for fats since they take too long to give the energy. Hence without Carbs, we feel tired. This also means that consuming carbs

before workouts is a hack to extend our duration and improve our performance by as much as 40%.

10. In order to burn fat: aerobic exercises are the best.
11. It's okay to work out in a cool environment because more sweat doesn't relate to weight loss (I personally prefer having sweat though since they're an indicator of being on track!).
12. Exercise can reset the rhythm of the glands which had gone haywire and hence treat deadly diseases like diabetes, heart attacks.
13. While exercising, one becomes susceptible to diseases and those micro-organisms floating around in the air, but in the long run, exercise strengthens immunity.
14. If ill and symptoms are below neck, avoid any exertion. If symptoms above head, light exercises might work.
15. Exercise reduces anxiety, and even heals wounds! (The only catch is people need to have faith in this power that they are born with, like Luke in Star Wars.)
16. Exercise boosts the memory power of the Brain by increasing a protein called BDNF. BDNF acts as a soil fertilizer for our brain, helping to really grow our neurons to large extent and form new connections.
17. Making changes in the lifestyle is hard, but doing so would enable us increase our BDNF and hence reap countless benefits.
18. Nothing in our body exists in isolation. One thing always impacts another. That's why having a healthy BDNF can help us master other spheres like depression, well being, and weight control.
19. Exercising daily, as opposed to alternative days, has more benefits. Stopping exercising means we nullify all the benefits we reaped and return back to baseline levels. But

starting again also restores those benefits; hence it's never a bad idea to start exercising.

20. Yoga acts as a good substitute to exercise, given that you're also performing the asanas which require some physical efforts as well. It is not just a substitute as it also enhances the mindfulness.
21. Maintain energy balance by not over eating and forgetting the diet aspect.
22. Leading a sedentary life, like being a "couch potato" in front of the TV, increases the chances of death by more than 61%.
23. Exercise not only helps us get rid of obesity but also delays aging, prevents cognitive loss and bone weight loss. This is the key every student needs to boost grades.

Module 3

SLEEP PILL

Chapter: 1

Introduction

"Sleep until you're dead," are the wordings I hear from the most creative species I am surrounded by. I have talked to numerous friends who claim that they have tons of work to do, which they often do at night: be it the assignment they have to turn in the next day, or pulling an all-nighter for the test. Some of us procrastinate our "morning work"; others are swayed by those who they admire the most: blindly following their idols. When I first watched the Iron Man 3, there was an instance where Tony (the main hero) describes how trivial sleep is for him as it was for Albert Einstein. The fact may not be true; however, it was sufficient to sway my puerile mind into believing in that idiosyncratic idea.

Although the contemporary world views sleep from the scientific constraints, history had quite a different lens. In the book Dreamland: Adventures in the Strange Science of Sleep, David Randall mentions that the Greeks regarded sleep as the middle stage between life and death, and also attributed it to sleep gods like Hypnos, Somnus, Morpheus. The ancient

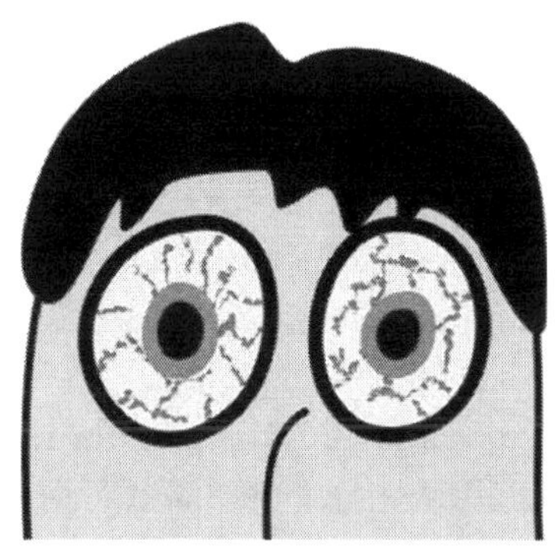

Egyptians made temples, where they engaged in hypnosis and dream interpretations. In the onset of the 1400s, there was the emergence of the scientific principles being linked to the concept of sleep. Some believed that it was triggered by a lack of oxygen to the brain, or it was caused by accumulation of toxic substances which withers off through sleep. They regarded sleep as an inhibitory reflex causing the body to shut down. Dreams, previously regarded to be of sacred origin, had started to become more of a subject of scientific analysis around the 1600s, as scientists like Marquis d'Hervey de Saint Denis and Alfred Maury began maintaining a daily record of their dreams without the intervention of any priest.

The start of 1900 marked an entirely new era, where new technologies and development of new methods refuted the scientific claims of the past. Universities like Stanford University began to record the sleeping patterns of individuals, especially children, and started observing variations based on geographical differences. In the later 1900s, the advent of artificial lights proved to be a game changer since people didn't have to vary their sleep cycles with varying day light durations. Sleep disorders started coming into the spotlight, and sleep research was growing more complex than ever: involving different other variables like aging, pain, circadian rhythm, etc.

Now the idea of sleep receives a great attention in the scientific world as it has shown its impacts in a broad spectrum: from our routine mental states on one end to even cancer at another end.

Let's zoom in on the idea of sleep. An average person, who sleeps around 7-8 hours of sleep a day, spends about a third of his life sleeping. And the notion of sleep is not limited to our species, rather it is persistent in every living organism, atleast to the complexity their body is designed for. For instance, even though cyanobacteria lack complex nervous systems like us in humans, they do exhibit the 24 hour inbuilt cycle/circadian rhythm, which is nothing but the natural 24 hour clock inside our body, making us drowsy around a particular time and helping us wake up. This cycle is not only limited to controlling sleep-wake time, but also impacts digestion, body temperature, etc. Even plants technically 'sleep' through this circadian rhythm as they cease to create energy at a point and turn on the energy consumption mode.

The sleep-wake regulation controlled by circadian rhythm is in itself composed of 2 different processes: Process S (sleep promoter) and C (sleep disrupter). The process S builds up throughout the day with its maximum intensity at night, which induces sleep. The process C also builds up throughout the day to maintain wakefulness; however, this declines at night so that it doesn't disrupt the process S's sleep inducing functions. Had the process not been there, we'd end up having a sleep schedule analogous to infants: no fixed time. We'd sleep in day, night, or whenever we feel like sleeping, and that slumber wouldn't be a continuous 6 hour sleep, it'd be more of intermittent 30 minute sleep naps.

STAGES OF SLEEP

If we analyze the notion of sleep as a monotonous entity, then we may be misguided. Rather, our sleep is divided into 5 distinct stages, each having its own peculiar importance. For fun fact, there's also a distinctive stage which is characterized by the occurrence of dreams. After going through all the 5 stages, we cycle back through all of them again, however, with varying durations than before.

Stage 1: This stage stimulates the sensation of drifting away from the present, where you start losing your individual identity, your muscles loosen up, and the brain's activity is reduced. This lasts for about 1-7 minutes and can be easily disrupted by an irksome sound. For a better mental model, this is you while traveling and your head starts leaning on the neighbor's territory without actively making any decision.

Stage 2: In this stage, the decline continues, which involves further slowing down of the eye movements, brain activity, heart rate, and body temperature. This is also a special stage because this is characterized by the presence of sleep spindles, which involve neural oscillations, and K complexes, which prevent any exasperating noises from waking us up. The exciting part here is that studies have shown that sleep spindles are shown to have a direct correlation with fluidic intelligence (which includes applying logic, reasoning, complex pattern identification), and its effects are even more pronounced when occurring faster, usually in later stages. K-complexes have also shown to play some role in memory consolidation. Its duration is about 10-25 minutes.

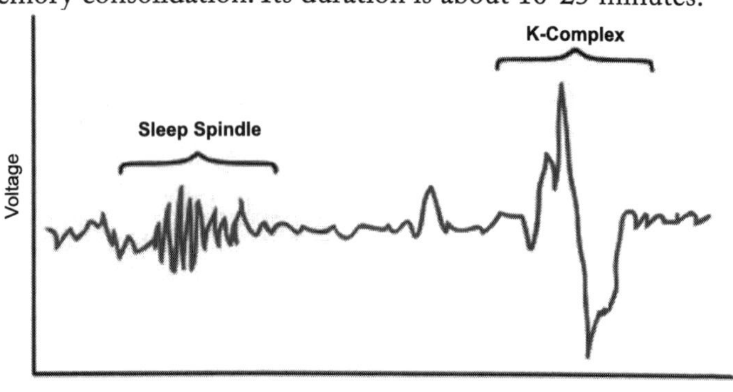

Stage 3 and Stage 4: The reason I mentioned both of them together is that they both are the constituents of the slow wave sleep. Though the third stage lasts for about 10 minutes, stage 4 constitutes about 15% of our total sleep time. It's the hardest to wake up in this state, so it's safe to consider that K-complexes are also the densest in this stage (and this is what the research says). One of things that fascinated me about this is that these stages are associated with memory consolidation properties, which we shall explore shortly.

Stage 5/REM (Rapid Eye Movement) period: This period is quite peculiar as compared to earlier stages. All the 4 stages described above can be grouped under one name of Non-REM sleep which is not categorized by eye movements. However, as the name suggests, in this stage, our eyes showcase rapid brownian movements. Not only this stage causes our eyes to display sporadic motion, but this also causes loss of muscle tone. And the most defining trait that distinguishes REM period from others is that this is when the dreams occur! Due to this reason, our muscles paralyze to prevent jumping into the middle of the night. Fun Fact: the individuals whose muscles don't immobilize experience disorders like sleep walking. Like its predecessors, REM period also follows the legacy by being involved in long term memory processing tasks. This was shown in a study which showed that students who took the examinations had longer REM periods than the baseline levels.

Up to this point, I wanted to enlighten the general idea of sleep and the charismatic effects it can have on learning. I shall explore the learning aspect a bit more in depth later, but for now, let's try to understand some fundamental differences in both of the sleep states.

Physiological Process	NREM	REM
Brain activity	Decreases from wakefulness	Increases in motor and sensory areas, while other areas are similar to NREM
Heart rate	Slows from wakefulness	Increases and varies compared to NREM
Blood pressure	Decreases from wakefulness	Increases (up to 30 percent) and varies from NREM
Sympathetic nerve activity (function to accelerate heart rate etc)	Decreases from wakefulness	Increases significantly from wakefulness
Muscle tone	Similar to wakefulness	Absent
Blood flow to brain	Decreases from wakefulness	Increases from NREM, depending on brain region

Respiration	Decreases from wakefulness	Increases and varies from NREM, but may show brief stoppages; coughing suppressed
Airway resistance	Increases from wakefulness	Increases and varies from wakefulness
Body temperature	Is regulated at lower set point than wakefulness; shivering initiated at lower temperature than during wakefulness	Is not regulated; no shivering or sweating; temperature drifts towards that of the local environment

The table above also makes sense since while we're dreaming, we seem to be in a state of illusion and fail to identify the differentiating line, and our body supports this state of illusion by shifting its responses much closer to the reality (And for a fun fact, dreams usually don't make sense because during that state, our emotional processing areas are active while our decision taking areas have suppressed activities causing bizarre and senseless dreams!).

EVOLUTION OF SLEEP THROUGHOUT HUMAN LIFE CYCLE

Like our body undergoes morphological changes, so does our sleep. This means the sleep an adult is getting must be very different in terms of the proportion of time spent in each of the above discussed stages and efficiency. In general, the sleep efficiency declines as we age. But this decline may not be very 'ideal', meaning that if not taken care of, this could occur at any age. In fact, I've met a girl, currently in college, who described her experience as "Regardless of when I sleep, at 12 or 2 in the morning, even if I am disturbed after 4 hours of sleep, I just can't fall back on bed." After I heard her, initially I thought she must be having an extreme hold on herself, but then I realized this isn't an ostentatious skill.

Infants/Newborns: At some point in our lives, we must have heard people say infants sleep a lot, like 16 hours a day. This sleep is distributed throughout the day with the longest continuous sleep being no greater than 4-4.5 hours. Their onset stages of sleep start with REM period instead of NREM. Instead of envying them, let's try to understand why they just don't sleep at night? The answer's straightforward: the circadian rhythm is not fully developed.

About 3 months in, and not only the circadian rhythm matures, but also the infants start shifting towards "normal" sleep cycles which include starting with NREM sleep, but the muscle paralysis is removed.

Young children: The number of hours is decreased; not only there are physiologic changes, but also social changes: school schedules, dark hours etc. They spend a longer time in the REM period and most of the sleep consists of stages 3 and 4. Also, by around 6 years, young children also begin to display circadian rhythm sleep preferences: of "night owl" or "morning bird".

Adolescents: Most researchers studying sleep changes in this age group underscore the importance of puberty changes more than that of the sequential flow of age. Even though adolescents require about 9-10 hours of sleep, most of the middle schoolers consistently fail to reach that hallmark. There is also a decline in the REM period; however, this issue can be mitigated by having a consistent bedtime.

Adults: There is another major transition in the sleep cycles of adults: they sleep and wake up earlier. This may be due to increased sensitivity towards light or advancement in the circadian rhythm pacemaker. They may experience brief interruptions close to REM period, and their slow wave sleep (SWS) declines 2% every decade (SWS is crucial for memory consolidation), and since it's hardest to wake up in the SWS, this may be another reason for frequent awakenings.

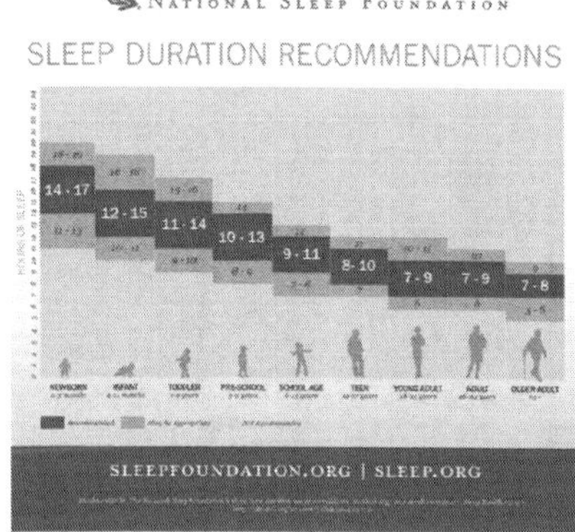

Chapter: 2

Dreams Are Real

I brought up the idea of dreaming earlier, about what REM sleep is known for, the dreaming stage and the paralysis of the body, but this is just half the truth. Dreaming is, in fact, not limited to being within REM sleep only; it also does occur in NREM periods, though the majority is backed in REM.

Like the concept of sleep, dreaming was also not interpreted without variations in judgments. Ancient Greeks and Romans believed dreams to be having some prophetic powers. Around the 19th century, people started coming up with their theories, some of those included that dreams allow us to fulfill repressed desires. After the technological advancement, scientists started believing dreams to be of no significance: they were thought as mere electrical impulses knitting random thoughts into a narrative. And it seems like this is what we all would consider to be dreams: fictional random thoughts with no significant relevance.

However, we humans have evolved into such convoluted beings that our bodies wouldn't expenditure energy with absolutely no purpose. In response to this, evolutionary psychologists proposed the "threat simulation theory" which describes dreaming to be an ancient defense mechanism to simulate the hostile situations allowing strengthening of neuro- cognitive skills for efficient coping tactics.

Numerous theories were formulated until recently, when the new research provides compelling co-relations between memories and those cherished sub conscious fantasies.

They predicted that the recalling of the dreams depends on the patterns of brain waves (which are usually of 3 types: alpha, theta, and gamma). Italian researchers conducted their studies on subjects by waking them up at various times and asking them to jot down their dreams, if any.

They concluded that participants who had the highest frontal theta activity had the highest recall rate. The interesting thing is that the activity of the exact same region is higher when we're self contemplating while we're awake or reviving the things that happened to us. This fact also cancels the notion of sleep as inhibitory reflex since these results convey that there's literally no difference in the sleep and the woken up state when we're dreaming or retrieving autobiographical memories.

However, we all must have had at least one dream that had such an intense impact on us, that we still can vividly describe it. At this moment, I can think of 4-5 dreams that really bewildered my senses. Researchers wanted to study this relation with the brain structure, and found out that these emotionally intense dreams are linked to parts of the brain responsible for emotion, and memory processing and consolidation: amygdala and hippocampus. This study is also backed up by another study which explained that people who have decreased REM periods fail to understand intricate emotions-crucial for social presence.

The studies took above points towards a crucial fact- Dreams help us process the emotions we experience while running our daily errands. To put it some other way, dreams themselves are not non-fiction; however the emotions those dreams carry are nothing else but what we experience while being awake.

DREAMS ACTING AS DUMBBELLS FOR OUR BRAINS: MAKING IT STRONGER AND STRONGER.

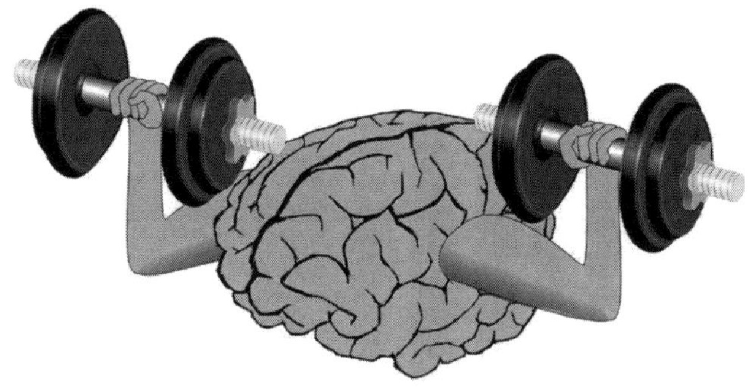

But again, is it possible to think that the content we dream would be picked by a randomizer picking some random thoughts from our brain and forming a happy ending (or spooky, maybe)?

The truth is dreams are related to what we do prior to sleep!

The researchers at Zurich center ventured to seek these answers by following the same experimental procedure as the Italian researchers did: wake up parti-cipants at regular intervals in the night and record what they've dreamt about. But this time, before going into sleep, participants completed a picture-word association task, requiring them to learn the associations and then assessed their memory. They not only found the positive correlation amongst those who had an uninterrupted sleep, but also in those who woke up at different points in the night.

It's obvious that the regularly disturbed participants had lower sleep efficiency than that of the uninterrupted ones, but they also found some intriguing results: there was no difference in the memory consolidation which reveals that sleep was able to perform unimpeded memory consolidation even after multiple awakenings. However, this does not mean to condense sleep timings because researchers also found another positive correlation: more the task (performed prior to sleep) related to the content of dream in NREM, better the learning. This means we also need to have some sufficient learning work to do before we sleep, to have sufficient amount of NREM sleep.

Dreams are more than just an illusionistic art; this is something we have established by now. They not only drive enhancement of memory recalls but also help to process the subjective feelings we experience.

Chapter: 3

Memory Enhancers In Sleep

In the first section, I brought up the presence of sleep spindles. These are transient brain signals that help to enhance our fluid intelligence. They're found in both light and deep sleep (Slow wave sleep), but recent studies have shown that they have a much higher density in the SWS as opposed to light sleep (even though its fundamental characteristics remained unchanged, shown in graphs B and C).

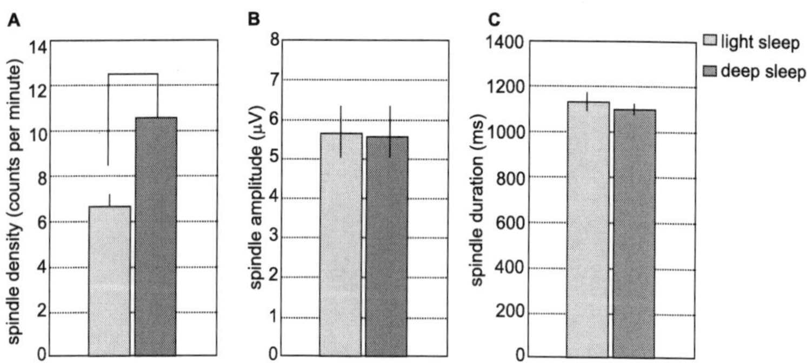

But if you remember, deep sleep is also the state of memory consolidation, so researches and experiments were conducted to see the relation between sleep spindle density and the subject's memory based on a test. The results were amazing: not only did they find that memory is directly related to sleep spindles, they also found a decrease in memory retention after deliberately reducing the sleep spindles (graph A below)!

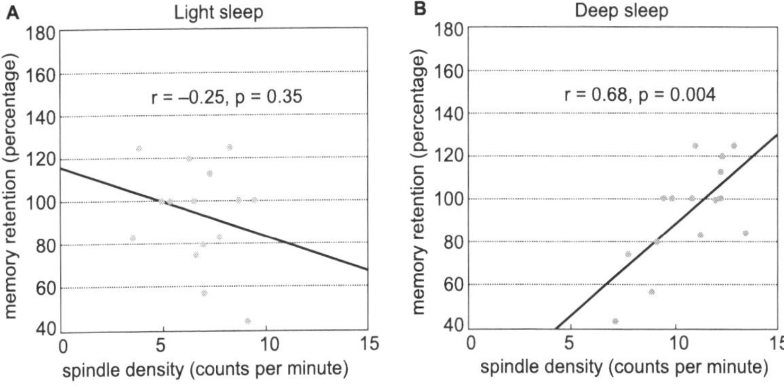

If you're a high schooler who normally struggles with memory retention, you must be feeling ecstatic at this point and must be wondering the stunts you'd have to undergo to cause this charismatic spindle density to increase.

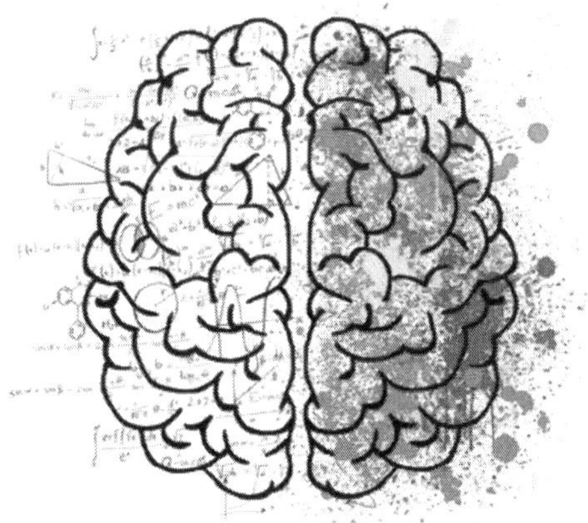

The most direct way is to spend more time learning novel things. Studies have shown that those who spend the time on learning before sleeping have higher density sleep spindles, than the non learners. If you zoom in at this point and try to put this and what we learnt about dreaming in the last section all together, it seems like dreaming also helps in memory consolidation and is related to what we do and experience prior to going to bed. So, is there any interdependence between sleep spindles and dreams as well?

It turns out that dream recall is in fact related to the density of our sleep spindles! And interestingly, this link appears to be even stronger in "bad dreams". The exact relation between them is not apparent but it does point to the fact that dreams may be under an influence of sleep spindles or they both may be the mechanisms for memory consolidation.

Sleep spindles are extremely important in our lives, and as we know nothing exists in isolation in our body, so seeking answers to this phenomenon might be analogous to a spindl-ey ride in itself!

Chapter: 4

Dethroned Royal Slumber

Reading about dreaming and pressing importance on the efficiency of sleep evokes a sense of self analyzing of our own sleeping state. And my intuitive statistics speak that most of the current readers were not satiated after reading about the benefits of sleeping. Rather, most will be having a moldy sense of the opportunities they have missed in such a long run.

The current lifestyle has already caused a disruption in the "ideal sleep" we all are longing to have. This condition does have a term of its own: Insomnia.

When someone's experiencing insomnia, the person may find it hard to fall asleep, difficulty in staying asleep, and easily able to wake up. Its impressions would reflect on the person's day's temperament, his work efficiency, and his drenched energy levels. This condition may be acute (short term) or chronic (long term) depending on the length of duration.

CAUSES

When asked the reason for lack of sleep, we generally transfer the worry by bringing the school work in the spotlight. But little do we know that this is the worst way of figuring out the root cause problems.

On the next level, I can go ahead and spill out a few factors:

Stress: Any cause of worry which diverts our psychic energy (consciousness) towards personal and social events.

Travel: This usually imparts an acute insomnia like symptoms due to jet lags. However, continuous late night/variable shifts can leave a chronic impact as well.

Poor sleeping habits: This involves going against your circadian rhythm and sleep-wake cycle by having a variable sleep-waking time, and napping at irregular intervals. This also involves having an inferior sleeping environment.

Heavy snacking before bedtime: Overeating before bed can cause a state of entropy.

Consumption of Caffeine, alcohol and drugs: Caffeine (giving rise to the infamous sodas and coffees) is consumed to get a boost. However, its intake before bedtime can interfere with our sleep cycles. In fact, taking coffee after afternoon causes sleep disorientations because of slow degradation of coffee.

Gadget usage before sleep: Blue light emitted from the electronic screen interferes with the production of melatonin hormone, the sleep inducer hormone.

But if I were to try to analyze to another level, the reason behind all these causes, I'd say lack of planning is a viable place to land. But this is not over yet. In the case of a disaster, the reviewing committee tries to get to the bottom by repeatedly questioning each and every level of cause. So if I question why do we not plan out, it seems like there's not enough self reflection.

But anyway, there are other factors as well which happen to interfere with sleep and facilitate development of insomnia:

Changes in health: Health entropy of any kind does produce a sense of restlessness causing our sleep to suffer.

Whatever may be the reason, the result is broadly the same: dissatisfaction with one's own life.

While the above discussed causes and effects were the extrinsic factors we're able to scrutinize, what about the changes that our glimmering eyes can't spot?

Apart from the imbalance in the hormones that play a direct role in regulating sleep- wake cycles; there are other hormones which seem to be impacted, the most common one being the Growth Hormone (GH).

Growth Hormones do what they sound like: bring in growth. Not only is this hormone the key behind our external body growth, this also is responsible for repairing any damaged tissue or muscle throughout our lives.

Research suggests that almost 75% of the total secretions of GH are secreted in sleep. There is a surge in its secretions in the 3rd stage or the slow wave sleep (about an hour after we fall asleep). However, if someone decides to pull an all-nighter, there will be no upsurge in that growth hormone. This is another factor which establishes the strong support towards the importance of sleep.

The key thing to note here is that this sleep should take place in relation to your circadian rhythm. This means that not sleeping when you're supposed to sleep will also result in suppressed GH secretions. Scientists conducted an experiment where they hid the subjects from the daylight and allowed them to have their own sleep schedules. Not getting environmental cues means that they could deviate from their regular sleep schedules. Testing their growth hormonal levels showed that not only they had suppressed secretions, but also had REM sleeps occur faster which means a shorter slow wave sleep.

GH is not only immensely important for adolescents, but also for adults and its importance even increases as its secretions decline with aging.

LOSS OF SLEEP AND OBESITY

There's an imbalance of hormonal secretions when there are casualties in sleep. But can those roots also reach obesity and weight gain?

Slow wave activity is a quantifiable character which gives an estimate how well our deep sleep is. This is usually low for people who're sleep deprived. Numerous studies have been conducted reflect that the decline in sleep hours corresponds to piling up of masses around our belly, and a similar relation is shown in the relation between attenuated sleep and diabetes. Analogous to growth hormone, there seems to be other hormonal participants in the disruptions as well, producing such sharp correlations. Ghrelin (the hunger hormone) and leptin (the satiating hormone) are 2 such players.

Under ideal conditions, Leptin levels are their maximum in the night and minimum in the mornings indicating a feeling of fullness at night. Ghrelin (which sharply declines after ingestion and builds up when hunger sets in) also has higher levels, though it declines by the second stage of sleep (its decline corresponds with the rise of leptin indicating leptin as the ghrelin suppressor), indicating we're usually hungry in the daytime and satisfied in the night. Since we have our maximum satisfaction levels in the night, we take in less fodder and hence need fewer measures to reduce the blood glucose levels. So, the insulin sensitivity is the lowest in the night to prevent falling of blood glucose levels (this goes back up by the morning as well).

However, in the sleep deprived state, leptin levels are at the lowest in the morning signaling body for unnecessary calorie intake. Even ghrelin is at high levels by 28% which even further support the hunger drive. This effect alone could be enough to prove the prevalence of obesity with the attenuating sleep hours, but there's more what is left.

Sleep deprived individuals are more likely to consume carbohydrates, the main traitors causing obesity as I talked about it in the diet module. This was proved in a study which showed short sleepers were more likely to embrace snacks than the regular meals, when both given in equal proportions.

Further our fitness goals could be even further 'overkilled' by this peculiar phenomenon: upsurge in insulin resistance by 40%. In normal conditions, our insulin sensitivity usually drops at night since our brain-the major glucose consumer- doesn't take in much of it and neither do our muscles. Not only does the brain intake fall, but the insulin release is also suppressed at night, and all these measures ensure stability in the blood glucose levels. In case of a sleep debt, all these effects persist throughout the day (as opposed to staying limited while sleeping) in their exponential form, leading to the development of one of the pre-markers of diabetes.

With the advent of technology, it seems like we've lost the harmonies connection we were born with our body. Adolescents have lost the sense of an ideal sleeping environment, which involves a dark and silent room persisting throughout the entire night. Their brains, after being hyper stimulated by the smart devices have reduced their sleep efficiencies, which studies show, is more or less has the same consequences of being sleep deprived (though in a slightly less pronounced way). What's further disturbing is that teenagers have even greater susceptibility to the negative impacts listed above since they usually show a difference of 2 hours between the slumber they get and slumber they're assumed to get. Yet, there seems to be minimal awareness of the devastating effects of missing this fantastical phase of life.

SLEEP AND AGING

Hormonal changes lead to physiological changes leading to obesity. But obesity also has its own peculiar inducing effects. Apart from the increased risk of cardiac diseases, sedentary life, and cognitive declines, there seems to be yet another impact: aging.

If you haven't heard of chromosomes yet, then in simple terms, they carry the genetic messages for all the features of our body: from our height, hair color to…literally everything. Chromosomes are passed onto progeny, they divide and what not. So, to protect these structures, there's some substance at its ends which are called telomeres. Studies have shown that the length of a telomere is an accurate indicator of our age. As we age, the telomeres deteriorate. This is very well depicted in the image below.

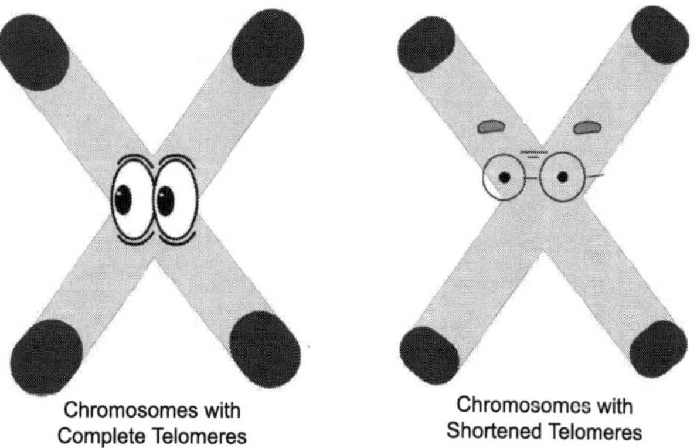

The thing is if there's shortened telomeres, there's less protection for the chromosomes (yellow colored in the above image) and hence the susceptibility of damage to their gene increases greatly (and genes constantly replenish our body's structural needs and every other thing including digestion). Not only there is increased susceptibility, the chromosome also loses its ability to divide hence there's no production of new cells. Slowing of new cell production directly leads to aging.

Studies have shown that people who are in sleep debt have shorter telomeres. And this shortening is also influenced by obesity. Sleep deprivation causes hormonal balance which causes obesity, and that directly speeds up aging!

Chapter: 5
Putting Things Together

The differences in sleeping patterns between the pre-industrial and post industrial phases are numerous. Our ancestors used to have longer sleep duration, which we all are well versed with. However, the modern human has evolved yet another way to cope up with this loss: by increasing sleep efficiency. Like high intensity exercises aids in burning significantly more calories in short durations, humans have increased their sleep efficiency by getting more done in less time.

For a moment it may seem like we've not only attained the pinnacle of sleep efficiency, but also managed to wither away the root causes of sleep distortion that has affected millions of our ancestors. This is true to some extent. When Homo sapiens lacked a physical solid shelter, they were endangered by the predation from wild beings, had a more noisy environment, and numerous other psychosocial stress factors that led them to have a decreased efficiency of sleep and also divert some consciousness towards being vigilant. Modern humans don't have to take that load. They have comfy beds, self controlled lighting and temperature, and physical shelter to avoid predation...What could possibly go wrong?

We fail to forget the "intelligent" phones which have penetrated so much in our human lives that often, we fail to be aware while using it. The blue light emitted by those 21st century gifts is horrendous for our sleep. We also cannot forget the other stresses that have become a second nature in our lives: economic hardships, social stress, discrimination, depression and whatnot.

Our sleeping environment thus, isn't perfect either. Variable or disruptive sleep environments wither away what our sleep is majorly based on: its efficiency. An inappropriate sleeping environment can ,more or less, produce the same results as those with sleep deprivation. Hence, in order to master the potency of sleep, gaining control over our sleeping surroundings is paramount.

CHERISHING ROUND AND ABOUTS:

If you've been having trouble sleeping lately, most likely you must have developed some unhealthy associations with it. By bringing slight changes to our room can actually trick our brain and prune all the negativity we've accumulated over years. Changes don't necessarily mean changing the physical characteristics of the room like its color; rather, it could be as rudimentary as rearrangement of the room items, clearing the mess, and associating our bed with only one task: Strong slumber.

After hacking the brain, gain control over the environmental characteristics. Ideally, our body temperature drops in earlier stages of sleep. So having a cooler, peaceful environment is not that much of a luxury. Light-whether artificial or natural- acts as external stimuli for our circadian rhythm and impacts the hormonal levels. Minimizing light levels simulates the dark environment and rules out the possibility of any hormonal imbalance. Also, for a fun fact, red lights act as a sleep inducer (I always wondered why all the brands had red light in their chargers).

Since technology has been so pervasive in human lives, it's hard to recommend ditching the tech use hours before sleep. To reduce the impact of blue light, installing some blue light filter applications should reduce its impact to some extent. I have a night mode feature built in my computer and phone which is set to auto turn on at as early as 7 in the evening. Before snoozing off, I put my phone in another corner of the room with Do Not Disturb mode to maintain sleep homeostasis.

MANAGING WHAT GOES IN

Rearranging our surroundings sounds plausible since it makes sense to alter the factors directly affecting sleep. But, managing what goes inside could baffle to some since it seems to have not even a slightest connection with our sleep quality. But, to reiterate, nothing related to our body exists in isolation: everything has its own *karma*. Under the insomnia section- loss of sleep and obesity part, I discussed that our insulin resistance increases by around 40% during the night, and the glucose metabolism falls. This is done to maintain the blood glucose levels throughout the night.

If you were to take in heavy glucose food in the night, with reduced insulin secretions and consumption and increased insulin resistance, it's very likely that it may produce hormonal imbalance interfering with our luxurious slumber.

Our intake in the afternoons or in general may be even less intuitive overall. But, if the impaired sleep schedule can cause impaired calorie intake through hormonal imbalance, doesn't it seem like there also exists a mechanism flowing the counter way?

Other substances like coffee are pretty obvious to be consumed since we usually drink it to ditch drowsiness. But the sky fact is coffees need to be refrained from consumption after noons because they contain caffeine, whose degradation is extremely slow which means it imprints lasting effects. In fact, even after not drinking coffee after noon, you'd still be having about half of the original caffeine remaining, though it wouldn't be much disruptive.

I like to save the coffee shots only for the real big days: only the crucial test days. Fun fact, I didn't even take coffee before writing my finals. This not only cushions my most lucrative period in 24 hours, but also averts the risks of developing its resistance, leading to addiction.

RAMBUNCTIOUS BLARE OF THE LITTLE CLOCK

Before snoozing off, you set tens of alarms, each lined one after another with a frequency of every minute, in an effort to just get you off the bed. As the first alarm goes off, our mind is dragged from the fantasy kingdom and a sense of anguish flows in since, we know the drudged cycle has started and wouldn't fade until you turn off those antichrist discos.

Alarm clocks are not the most liked invention of all time. Yet, we bet our life on them for waking up on a regular day, even before an early morning flight. But there's some concreteness behind the reason our brains consider the alarm clocks to be rowdy.

As soon as the blaring alarm goes off on its maximum volume, our Brain perceives this as a shock, prompting us to immediately be on our toes. The reason why we normally don't have such an abrupt reaction is because we've been habituated to the sound of an alarm clock as a non threatening sound (you can experiment by setting a random alarm tune and analyzing the change in your response). This response is much like the one we'd have in a threatening situation that would cause an increase in our blood pressure. Several people have reported to have mild headaches persisting for about an hour as well.

The best path to take is trust your gut. The built in circadian rhythm we're equipped with is intricate enough to help us wake up at the time we should be waking up.

But in the contemporary hustle, it becomes hard to rely on your instincts. The ideal way is to raise the bar gradually. There are some apps which have these smart alarm mechanisms that steadily raise the alarm's volume, or use the natural sounds. Another option is investing in sunrise alarm clocks that gradually light up your room mimicking the sunrise. This has great potency in maintenance of our circadian rhythm.

However, if cost is a factor, then sticking to nature like smart alarms is also potent to some extent. I have been having a phenomenal experience with these alarms so far as this kind rejuvenates my spirit every single morning.

SHREDDING SWEAT AND SLEEP

The bodily movements which strip the sweat and the pounds off our body may be influencers for our slumber as well. However, it's isn't that apparent. While some researchers claim it triggers the emergency response in our body which produces antagonistic effects, some seem to counter this notion. The saying "If you believe it, you get it," produces this charismatic effect here.

Studies have proved that the individuals who perceive they are being tired and are going to rest well after a heavy workout do end up having a better and faster sleep. This can be explained as a consequence of the placebo effect. Another explanation to this positive relation may be due to the tiredness after workouts.

However, if you're a naturally morning-working out person, then it's not so gloomy for you as well: Researchers at Northwestern University have figured that exercising in the daytime is more efficient than dusk hours, involving our ability to use oxygen. However at the end of the day, consistency is what I'd stress the most on.

I have been doing 9pm workouts since 2018, and I have never been more happier. I tried morning and evening schedules but I figured that those periods were most prone to be clashed with any other activity, making my workout time malleable. However, it is imperative to have the least malleability in the workout schedules to effectively shred and maintain weight, which I have discussed in the Q and A section too.

BRAIN HACKING TO PRODUCE PROFOUND RESULTS

This 3 pound organ of skill in our body is the center of all the processes and phenomena in the body. If we one can perform actions that can influence our body, life, as well as sleep, it would be immensely gratifying.

The first thing over here is the brain's associations. Making the brain associate the bed with the task of sleeping only can produce charismatic results. This means that the only activity which you'd be doing is diving into that deep slumber. This leads your brain into associating the bed with the task of sleep, so as soon as you slide in, your mind would sub consciously slide into sleep. After gaining the consciousness of this subtle trick, initially I had actively made efforts to prune my habit of lying on the bed apart from the dusk, and I don't regret even a bit of it.

After having a control over the stimulus, it's also imperative to note that just avoiding using the bed wouldn't produce its effects if you start taking mid day naps.

Lastly, there's still scope to gain further boost in the sleep even when once you're in the bed. This method is called **Progressive muscle relaxation** and has positive reviews from people who previously suffered from insomnia.

The technique derives its roots from relieving muscular stress and thus reducing anxiety. But the key is it needs to be envisioned and not be done physically.

Start by diverting your consciousness towards your muscles individually and contract them for 5-10 seconds. While contracting, create an imagery of the tension also being squeezed out. This envisioned efflux of stress has slumber inducing properties.

Generally, I manage to have an efficient sleep without using progress muscle relaxation. However in the times of distress, I find no better path to turn to.

Chapter: 6

Personal Trajectory

After watching Iron Man 3, I was set towards sleeping only 3 hours a year. Seriously. I tried, but thought I wasn't worthy. I had been a game addict back in the days, slept around 2 in the night with an ultra variable schedule, and even witnessed my efforts to undo it all turning futile. Even after entering 10-11th grade, when I was out of the vicious circle, I failed to realize the paramount role of proper sleep.

However, researching for this chapter has been one of the best decisions I have ever made. Not just I was ecstatic about writing it, I also got involved into writing academic papers in this context.

As I implemented these techniques, I was able to make changes that actually helped to break and rewire the habit loop. I now associate my bed with its only primary task: Sleep. Also, based on this association principle, I managed to link different corners of my house with different activities (I discussed my sleep schedule in the Q and A section).

Muscle relaxation techniques seemed to prune away the pain and helped me sleep before the big days, and consistency in my sleep schedule has made my waking up process seem trivial.

Making these changes require some use of our psychic energy. However, once invested, it'll save all the energy being drained in depression, anxiety like symptoms.

My alarm clocks now have their chirp which I had been with since my childhood, and the hormones seem synchronized with what my mind dictates. Most importantly, I now rejoice in my fantasy moments like never before!

Takeaways

1. Sleep is the most ignored element out of all the fundamental elements, even though this is something of paramount importance.
2. Every organism has its own internal clock, making changes to have the maximum productivity in the tasks we do at various times of the day.
3. Our sleep cycle is classified into discrete stages with each one having its own importance. For example: memory formation, dreaming.
4. Dreams have their own purpose, helping us to process complex emotions required in our life. They also help in memory formation.
5. PRO TIP: If you want to remember or learn something by heart, learning before going to bed can make your dream come true!
6. Sleep spindles are what help remember complex situations, lessons we study in our lives. To maximize these spindles, the best way is to keep exploring and learning!
7. Insomnia is a condition associated with difficulty in sleeping, commonly caused due to poor lifestyle trends.
8. Insomnia extends its roots to more aspects apart from disrupting our sleep cycles. These include reducing our body's growth, enhance aging, and cause obesity.
9. Our sleep cycles can be set back to the reset mode, and the key lies in improving our sleep environment and lifestyle changes.

Module 4

THE GRAND PILL

Chapter: 1

One Size Doesnt Fit All

After all the theory and the pieces of advice that you got so far, I wouldn't be surprised if there's a question hovering in your mind. 'Alright, Mridul, we know all the theory parts you have gone along so far, but how to put that theory in practical usage?' Before I increase any more suspense, in this section, I will be guiding you on how to develop a weight loss plan. Let me clear here of why I am not actually telling you the exact "exact plan" which I personally used to lose weight. Each one of us has a unique body, a different schedule, a unique lifestyle, and ,of course, individual preferences. After so many peculiarities amongst us, it's hard to design a one-size-fits-all plan and hope it would be working flawlessly for everybody. Of course, I would be sharing my essential tips and strategies as well, which I personally used, but I want you to use it as an example and also probably experiment it in your own lifestyle to see how well it works on you.

I again want to remind you that this section is not a weight loss program or anything, it basically teaches you how to be self-accountable, and it allows you to create a schedule that you can stick to in the long run. And to give you a little disclaimer here, you want to have a plan that can be followed in the long term because weight loss is supposed to be a gradual process in which the graph of weight slowly and steadily goes down. Right now, you might be like "Slow and steady wins the race is true only in stories and not in the advanced world we're currently living in" but I discussed in the diet section why it's the only way ahead. So long story in short, after this section, you will be having a weight loss plan ready-designed, just by you and only for you.

Before beginning your planning, I want you all to keep one thing in your mind: this planning will require you to set many goals that you have to continually achieve to hold yourself accountable and on track. Setting goals are paramount to attaining your endeavors, and in this case, it's a fitness journey. And I want you to understand that those goals must be SMART. To elaborate,

S- Specific

M-Measurable

A-Attainable

R-Realistic

T-Time Based

For specific goals, I mean that you should be crystal clear on what your motives are, as in why you are doing this in the first place. Identifying answers to such questions will make you perform much better than you would if you just write weight loss as the only goal. For example, before starting, I knew I was losing weight so that I can apply for the exchange program again next year, and initially, I had a goal of losing 10 kilos, coming to 75 kg.

Next is measurable. Being able to assess your progress towards your goal allows you to do further planning towards it and also opens the opportunity of making modifications to them. If weight loss is the goal, measuring your weight regularly makes you more committed to the journey.

Attainability gives you a sense of whether your goals can be achieved by you or not. Being able to visualize yourself, achieving your goal will make you more committed to it. However, this doesn't mean anyway that you set easy goals. Studies have shown that you are more likely to achieve a goal that challenges you than that with an easy target.

Do your goals make you feel like they are unrealistic? In today's world, it's so hard to call something unrealistic just by looking at it. But to reduce the anxiety of following them, you want to break your goals into many subunits, which appear less daunting. For example, I didn't start my weight loss journey by deciding to lose 25 kilos at all. I had a big plan to lose 10, which I broke it down into 5+5 i.e. setting goals for losing 5 kilos and then executing it for another 5.

The last is time-based. You want to set deadlines that prevent you from procrastinating for your goals. For example, I set 4 weeks to lose 5 kilos. This way, even if I had the days when I exercised less, it made me find the time in the days when I could compensate for the time.

SMART goals are crucial to help you stay focused on the plan of action you create. So, now is the time to write down this acronym– SMART on the left side of the paper before anything else, which will keep you reminding of your motive.

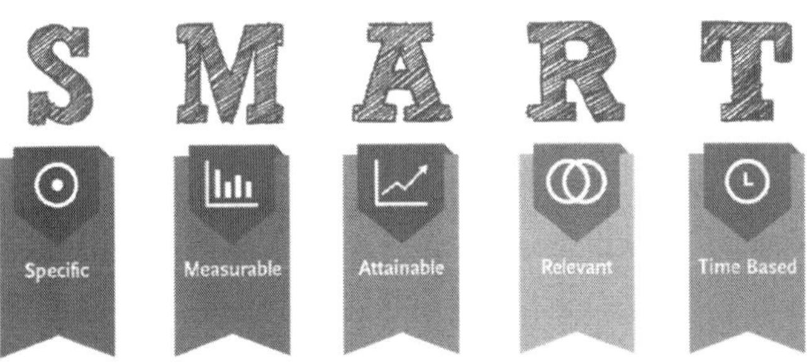

Chapter: 2

Shooting For the Bullseye

We all have heard the famous quote by Lao Tzu that "A journey of 1000 miles starts with a single step." This weight loss journey is no less work, and I am sure everyone realizes it well (if you didn't, you wouldn't have come here :)). The first step towards this journey would be figuring out what your goal weight is. Now this goal weight should match the standards of what we discussed in the SMART goals section to increase the probability of achieving them. There are 4 steps involved in doing so:

1. The first thing I want you to do is to rewind and think, what was your highest weight of all times in your life? Once you figure out the answer to this, there are 4 other things you need to do and write them down on a piece of paper (preferably a diary because you want to keep track of it) and label it as "HIGH":

   - How did you physically feel at that weight?
   - How did you emotionally feel at that weight?
   - What kind of comments did your friends and the

family make at that time?

- What medical problems did you face then?

2. The second thing to do is to think about what your lowest weight was of all times? After you have the answer with you, repeat the steps you followed in the first part and write down all the 4 answers and on the top label it as "LOW".
3. The next thing required is to figure out the weight where you keep coming back to with no change in your diet and exercise. This weight could be the one in which you currently are in, or probably most of the time, so figuring this out shouldn't be a big deal. Label it as "STABLE".
4. The last thing to do is to calculate your ideal weight. Now, this is not what the goal weight is, ideal weight is something that can be calculated with a mathematical formula. In this case, I am going to use the "Hamwi method". Basically, what you need to remember is that for a male who is 60 inches tall (5 feet), the ideal weight is 106 pounds. So, every inch over 60 inches would add 6 pounds to 106. For example, a guy who is 5 feet 10 inches (70 inches) would have an ideal weight of 166 pounds. For females, this formula has slight variations. A female who is 60 inches tall must have a perfect weight of 100 pounds. Every inch above 60 adds up 5 pounds. So a female who is 5 feet 10 inches would have an ideal weight of 150 pounds.

After you have written all this in your diary, you need to select a goal weight that is in the range of weights between the stable weight and the ideal weight. Keep one thing in mind: your goal weight shouldn't be less than the perfect/ideal weight, though it can be in the 10-pound range of your stable weight.

Now that you have set your goal weight, the next thing you should do is to share this goal with someone in your family or your good friend who can keep you accountable and bring you on track in case of any deviation from your goal.

After this, the time frame is the next item to write in your diary. How fast do you want to lose weight? Let's say your goal is to lose 15 pounds of weight. A realistic short term goal would be to lose 1 pound per week, and hence your long term goal would be 15 weeks in total to reach your target.

Another thing I would personally recommend is, if the difference between your current weight and the goal weight is too significant, consider breaking down the goal into smaller checkpoints. Earlier, when I was at 85 kilos, I never imagined that I'd lose 23 kilos even in my wildest dreams. I first started by setting my long term goal as losing 5 kilos in a month. Thus, my short term goal was to lose 1 kilo (roughly 2 pounds) every week. After that, I kept on achieving my checkpoints, which were marked on the intervals of 5 units and I stopped around 62. This way, I had complete control over my journey; when to start, slow down, and end, which is something I aim to teach you through this book. Please keep in mind that losing a kilo a week is not necessary and is usually not recommended as well because weight loss needs to be gradual and not in a rush. I did so because getting rejected from a scholarship worth $25,000 just because of these cursed pounds isn't fun, right?

Once you have written down everything in your diary, I want you to understand why, how, and when to weigh yourself. Whenever I used to stand on that rugged machine (or that's what I used to call it back in the time), it would always be during the medical test in my school. This was a compulsory test for every kid to take until 9th grade, where they would weigh you, measure your height, and check your eyesight with a frequency of once every year. Trust me, whenever I used to be in the queue waiting for my turn to come, I would always be worried about what number that wicked scale was going to show up at that time. Would I have an increment by 5 kilos (that was usually the case), or those digits would have come up with a new attack plan at that time? And trust me on this, it wasn't just me, it was all of my friends.

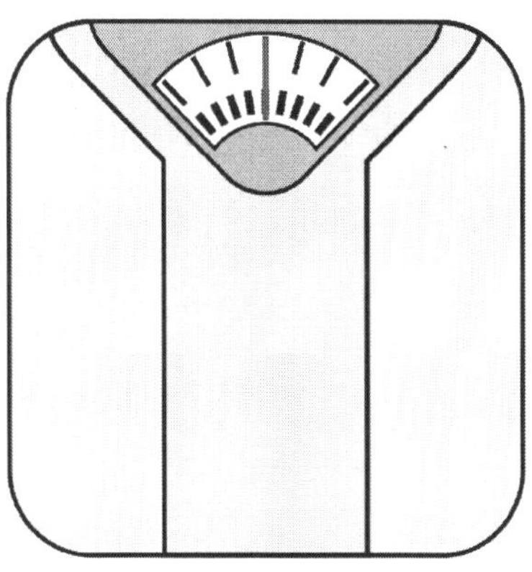

Now, if I look back at that, those rugged machines were the only ones which used to show me the real reflection of where I was and before standing on those were actually the ONLY TIMES I used to worry about turning out overweight (even though I always had been and I knew that). So weighing yourself is a significant part of your journey.

But if you are starting your weight loss journey and somebody sees you weighing yourself, chances are they might ask you to stop doing so or else you would get too carried away by numbers and get distracted from the primary goal(At least that's what I had heard from my parents when they saw me weigh every day). But a recent 2-year study, in which 162 overweight and obese gym members were asked to consider them every day and keep a note of their progress, showed that the subjects were more likely to lose weight with self-monitoring without any adverse psychological effects.

So, therefore, is it HIGHLY recommended to weigh yourself every morning. A couple of other things to keep in mind are as you stand on the scale, look straight ahead to a single point, count up to 3, and then step out and check your weight. If the above steps are not done accurately, chances are the weighing scale might show some small variations in its results either positively or negatively (sometimes even bigger), which can make you unrealistic about your goals, and that is the last thing that must happen with you. So give some time to the scale and ensure that the weighing machine is kept on a hard surface and not on carpet.

If you keep recording your weight every day, most likely, you will find some fluctuations in your weight, and that's completely normal! This may be because of slight changes in your day to day habits or your diet. These fluctuations become trivial if you are accomplishing your short term goals ie, shedding 1-2 pounds a week.

Initially, I started weighing myself with the classical weighing machine (non-digital) at the same time of the day: as soon as I got out of bed. This way, it basically became an automatic response for me to weigh myself, and hence, I didn't need a reminder for doing it. And doing it in the morning also enabled me to plan my rest of the day.

But do keep in mind that people who are suffering from eating disorders shouldn't weigh themselves every single day since that can lead to even lesser food consumption, which could be dangerous.

Chapter: 3

Planning is Everything

Planning is everything.Even a child gets it. I am sure this is THE one task everyone must have done before and might feel like to skip over this section, but before you do so, WAIT! Like I had said earlier, we tend to try out a lot of different techniques -some fails and some works - but knowing an exact plan ready in front of you is not at all a bad idea. Plus you also get to know how I had solved this problem (which is the entire point of the book), so go ahead and gain as much as you can out of it.

If you remember from the exercise chapter, I had mentioned the energy balance: the positive and the negative balance. The energy balance is, in fact, the key to weight loss. If calories taken in are equal to the calories used up, a person's weight remains the same.

Any alterations in this balance cause fluctuations in the weighing scale. I also mentioned that there are two ways to have a negative energy balance: one is to increase the energy expenditure, and the second is to cut down calorie intake. In this section, I am going to discuss the first method, which is,

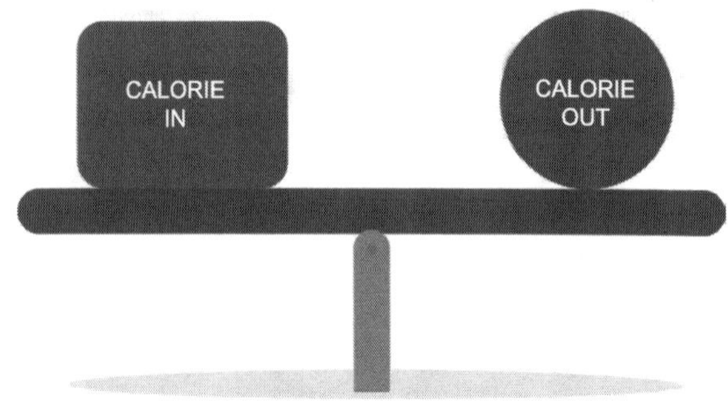

designing a plan to increase energy expenditure with the help of exercise. But a DISCLAIMER before you take out your diary and start scribbling. We all have heard of stories of people who regain weight after losing and then spread the word, 'Just don't lose weight in the first place (yes, I have received such advice!). They will tell you the entire sad story of how they regained weight, but what those "advisors" wouldn't say is whether they were keeping up with their training or not. So, I want you to come with an exercise plan that needs to be maintained for pretty much the entire lifetime. I don't want to be misunderstood here that only one single plan needs to be maintained for the whole life, instead keep in mind that the frequency of making changes to plan should be low which would allow this to become a part of your life. Now you might be like, "But what to do if we get deviated from our plan?" The answer is, of course, there will be sick days and the holiday break where you just can't stick to your plan. But what is more important is to come back to your routine. I know it will be a little harder but JUST DO IT.

You need to start with planning out 3 factors: the Duration, Intensity, and Frequency of exercise. Starting off with the duration, the Academy of Nutrition and Dietetics Evidence Analysis Library says that the amount of activity required for weight loss is 150-420 minutes per week. Duration is directly related to weight loss, that is, greater the period, more the pounds shred. Personally, when I was exercising to lose weight, my duration used to vary between 30-40 minutes per day, making 210- 280 minutes on a weekly basis.

The next thing to play with is the intensity. To figure out which exercise works out as the best for you, just try a bunch of different exercises with varying intensity and see how you feel after doing the exercise. Do you feel satisfied after doing the exercise? Do you automatically prefer one particular activity, or is it just because you had heard about your friend's cousin's aunt's kid losing weight by this specific exercise? Or is it you feel the training is a lot more vigorous, and it just isn't enough to get your heartbeat a little faster because you can't do it well? If unable to perform the exercise in the right way is the issue, I'd say try learning it from online sources like YouTube where you actually see a person perform that particular exercise. But if this doesn't work, I cannot stress more on the importance of finding tasks that you find leisure in because, in the end, exercise needs to be enjoyable for long term sustainability.

And instead of sticking to one particular exercise and doing it over and over again, I would suggest having a fixed combination of activity that you would be doing. So let's say you like crunches and running, then I would do running for a while, switch to crunches and come back to running. This basically needs to be done in one workout session. For example, I like jumping (without a rope) and high knee running. So, for almost my entire weight-loss period and even now, I primarily stick to these 2 exercises and would switch between the two in a single session. Also, I did a comparative study in which I found that a mixed intensity exercise is the best for maximum memory benefits, so coming up with a combination of activities that do not belong to the same intensity category is highly recommended.

At this point, if you are one of those (like me) who find it too hard to find the "right fit" for yourself, the best advice I can give you is Go ahead and create your own exercise! I am not asking you to start from scratch and apply rocket science; all I am asking you is to just change a few parts of the "pre-defined exercises" and then enjoy the exercise. The main essence of a workout is to get your heart racing- if that new hybrid exercise routine you just made does that, you're good to go! For example, if you noticed earlier, I mentioned rope skipping without a string, which might seem boggling. I personally enjoyed jumping but hated the thing with rope- because whenever that wicked rope gets entangled with your feet, you just have to stop and start over and over again, thereby reducing productivity. What I did was I mimicked my hands as if they were holding ropes and jumped and simultaneously rotating my full arms. This way, I could do it for longer without any disturbance and also ensure I had the exact same body movement! See, THAT'S HOW THE WORLD WORKS.

The final thing to plan is the frequency. This refers to how many times you will exercise in a week. During my weight loss days, I used to work out all 7 days a week, again for the same reason: to lose weight ASAP! And I will also recommend this to those of you who are hyperactive and excited to lose weight. Generally, those who start off too fast usually tend to slow down by the end; so basically, you want to ensure you are getting the most work done in the period when you are in your fastest mode.

If you are one of those who is wondering whether or not to count the minutes of moderate and vigorous exercise equally, let me tell you: that's a good question! Of course, if you work hard, you are rewarded more, and so is the case in exercise. Basically, every one minute of vigorous exercise counts as 2 minutes, and every minute of moderate exercise counts as 1 only. So let's say you jump for 20 minutes a day (that's precisely what I did and still do); thus, your total exercise time will be counted equivalent to 40 minutes! So, if you remember I had told you earlier that I exercised 210-280 minutes weekly, it was only partially true. Out of my 30-40 minute workout per day, I would devote around 25 minutes to just jumping. So, my total time of exercise used to range between **385-455 minutes weekly.**

Putting up the pieces together:

1. Choose an activity or a combination of activities that works out for you (preferably a combo with mixed intensities).
2. Determine its intensity, duration, and the number of days you would be exercising per week.
3. Make sure you reach the limit of at least exercising 150 minutes per week (this is after counting the time of vigorous exercise as double the actual time).

I also suggest keeping notes of some tips you find helpful and do write your goals in your diary. For example, if you decide to bike and jump 5 days a week, you can make notes like: "I will bike for __3__ days for __40_____ minutes per session at _____moderate_____ intensity and jump for _____2___ days for _____15____ minutes per session which is always at high intensity. This workout takes 180 minutes of exercise a week. You can always tune-up this template for your personal, customized workout regime.

MAKING OUT TIME:

So now we have understood how to make our planner for exercise, but guess what, that is only 50% of the whole. Let me break it down for you: planning was one thing, but finding the TIME for executing the plan is another. And, we all know the only thing that keeps us from being the perfect human on this planet is more time. "How to find the time to do all this extra work if we already have a long to-do list for the day?" Honestly, I had faced this challenge as well before starting to lose weight, and every time anyone would ask me why I don't exercise, I would excuse myself by saying, "I am in class 10, how in the world am I supposed to have extra time?"

But, it turns out after I started, I could find time for my exercise routine even during my final board examinations! And now, I am going to tell you how to do that and how I did it.

Firstly, you need to creatively start thinking about how you can slide in those 30 minutes in your day for the exercise, regardless of other things; that means be it an exam tomorrow or whatsoever, those 30 minutes need to be there. Take it this way, prioritizing workout usually can be your last option: you will easily find tons of excuses to just not do it. But try out this technique: schedule your exercise on your calendar as if it is the appointment or some big day for you, and make sure to keep this appointment ON THE SAME TIME every single day. Let's say on Monday you do the exercise in the morning, so try to do your exercise pretty much at the exact same time in the upcoming days. Trust me on this technique, since this is basically like a coding exercise for your subconscious mind so that you never need to be reminded of it. If you think, on the other days you will not be able to find time because of work or some other stuff, therefore just keep this thing in mind before deciding the time for your exercise.

The second tip, which I personally find as the MOST crucial advice, is trying linking your workout to some task you perform every single day. For example, we all usually start the day by brushing. So, if you decide to set your exercise time somewhere in the morning, try doing it right after brushing. This way, you will be much more likely to do exercise than you would do so at a random time.

If you would genuinely follow these 2 basal steps, you would be able to glide through this barrier! Since I had my school and other stuff going, there was no way I could find time for exercising in the morning or afternoon (although I tried my best to have maximum physical movement possible). In the evenings, I had extra classes, so no evening time was free as well. But there's one slot I found which worked perfectly well for me, even today: the 9-9:30 pm slot. Now why just this particular time? So here's my secret to exercising: I exercise while watching my favorite show, "Aladdin - Naam Toh Suna Hoga".I take this TV show very seriously because I am its biggest fan ever! So, this slot already resembles something like an appointment slot wherein I do no other work except watching this show: even if I had my board exam the very next day. Secondly, I linked my exercise to something that I watched in a routine with genuine love, so it automatically reminded me to work out. But this doesn't take 30-40 minutes, right? Well, the remaining 10-15 minutes I used to find in my study breaks and in the time between coming back from school and the extra classes. Although if you remember the night time exercises have a lesser amount of benefits than the morning ones, still something's better than nothing!

GETTING MAXIMUM MINUTES IN THE LEAST MINUTES:

After knowing how to make the time out, there's, in fact, another tactic that can enable you to MAKE THE MOST IN THE LEAST AMOUNT OF TIME. If you keep exercising and not lose weight, that would be the biggest de-motivation leading to burnout. And this leads to my next important tip: if you are doing a combo of exercises, try to devote the most time you can to vigorous activities (but also don't forget the moderate ones, please). When I used to watch Aladdin show, I would do nothing else but just jump: on and on straight for 20-25 minutes. And in the remaining time, in between my study breaks, I would do high knee running on the spot, which is a relatively less vigorous exercise. On top of that, I commuted between my home and school on my cycle, which also counts as that of a moderate intensity.In this way, I was able to get the "maximum minutes in the least minutes" (since vigorous counts as double the time).

SAFETY PRECAUTIONS

The final and the most critical thing in this section is safety. This should not be a surprise that safety comes first before everything. If you want to lose weight, you want to make sure that you stay safe so that you can stay persistent on your goal without any breaks in it. Hence, make sure of some of the following points:

1. Make sure you warm up before starting out for an intense exercise (I usually do a little bit of stretching).
2. Give yourself time to cool down.
3. Always hydrate yourself with plenty of water before starting to exercise, and if the workout lasts longer than 45 minutes, make sure to drink water in sips during exercise as well.
4. Plan your outdoor days according to the temperature outside. Avoid going out on the hotter days (To know how I solved it, refer to the extra Q & A chapter).

Chapter: 4

Strategies for Eating Out

"So, you want to order from BTW even though you are trying to lose weight?" That was the first reaction my mum had on her face when I asked her if I could order from my all-time favorite restaurant. We all have some favorite food without which we just can't seem to last long (at least, I definitely do). But between grabbing our favorite food and us, there's only one thing: THE MASSIVE WEIGHT LOSS PLAN that we are committed to. Now, we all want to lose weight, but the fact that eating from a restaurant would cause hindrance is also no surprise. It turns out that there's a way with which you can prevent yourself from staying away from your dream dish for long.

The first tip is to avoid as much as you can. The more you can hold yourself away from those things, the better it is. So, if you are in a school or a place that has cafeterias, just try carrying your own lunch as much as you can. You will find yourself in situations where your friends bring those lucrative items like chips, burgers, and whatnot, and you are having a hard time controlling yourself (I would always find myself at such situations when at school).

Speaking from personal experience, your conscious mind

would still be trying to remind you of your weight loss goals, but on the other hemisphere, it would be doing the calculations of how much more workout you would have to do to compensate and would be convincing you to simply go ahead and eat it. The best way out of this situation is by having your own snack! As simple as it sounds, this can add weight to your conscious mind debate arguments and help you survive the debt of extra workout you were about to take. Now having fruits as snacks should always be your first priority, but sometimes to add enough weight to end the argument, you need something a little salty and a little crunchy. So, I would also recommend that having some salted peanuts or some fox nuts with you isn't a bad idea.

By reading the above paragraph, the only assumption you might be making right now is that I am asking you to become reclusive. The answer is no. Eating with friends is one of the most joyous moments of life. Then, how do you deal with it when you actually go out and eat at the restaurant? Well, there's a saying that goes like, "Failing to plan is planning to fail." With planning, you can steer through anything. Before anything else, just make sure you plan your visits well.

I am going to discuss some strategies you can follow before, while, and after your outing.

BEFORE GOING TO THE RESTAURANT:

1. You can try to cut down 100-150 calories per day, 3 days before the planned event. This will help you make 300-450 calories available for the big day.

2. Additionally, you can increase your exercise time by 10-15 minutes from 3 days before, which would add more to your savings account.
3. The next thing you need to do is if you are meeting up with your pals, TAKE THE LEAD AND DECIDE THE RESTAURANT. Doing this will not only enable you to pick up the place that matches what you need but also allows you to research their menu in advance so that you are not caught up in the debate again when standing in the queue for an order. Now, this might sound like a lot of hard work, but instead of looking up every new place you go, just stick to the ones you like the most. For me, it was BTW and Pizza Hut. For Pizza Hut, there aren't many options of what you can call "Healthy" as the name says, but in BTW (which I more often stick to) has tons of food options.
4. You also want to make sure you are going with a small group of people. This just reduces the chances of you being under peer pressure and eating something you will regret later on. To expand on this, a study was conducted to check the influence of eating companions on people. 70 women pairs were chosen, and their behavioral mimicry was analyzed by counting the number of bites they took. The number of bites they took was categorized into 2 subcategories: mimicked bites (bites made within a 5-second interval when another person took a bite) and non-mimicked bites (bites taken later than the 5-second range). It was found that women took more mimicked bites than the non-mimicked bites. Considering this, a large group of people would result in significantly higher mimicked bites, leading to overeating. Hence it is advised to keep the group small.
5. The last and the most important thing is to check your hunger scale before leaving out. When I say check, I literally mean say out aloud to your body, "How hungry are you?" The point is you don't want to go with the emptiest

belly possible as this would lead to over-eating at the food place. Make sure you feel healthy, not too empty, but not too full: The Middle Path.

AT THE RESTAURANT: Now you have reached the place for which you have been working harder for the past 3 days. Now what?

1. Be the first one to order. As I said earlier, with peer pressure, being the first to order would prevent you from coming under the influence of what your friends would buy.
2. Always ask for some extra salad, and ask them to put sauces and the gravy on one side if they can. This way, you can control how much of it you are taking.
3. Finally, just keep asking yourself at some intervals about the hunger level. Just stop eating as soon as you start to become full and ask for a packing box if available. But, remember to avoid eating as much as you can.

AFTER THE RESTAURANT: Now that you have fulfilled what you wanted the most, you want to make sure that this wasn't devastating for your goal.

So, for the next 3 days, do the same drill: cut down 100-150 calories a day, and increase the exercise time for 10-15 minutes a day.

This might sound like a ton of work, as a cherry on top of the already current work you have. But, it's harder to get started, and once it has been started, this should just flow with your wind. In the initial days, in my free time, I want you to reflect on what you have learned out of this, and write 3 strategies on your own in your diary in all 3 scenarios (before, at, and after the restaurant) about what works out the best for you to avoid deviation. Writing this down enables the material that you have learned and pondered upon to resonate with your subconscious thought process.

Chapter: 5

Hunger Intensified

Timing is everything…Even a child gets it. Yet, as I look around, I find most of us have a skewed sense of when our body actually cries for meals. Just like we humans have an extraordinary ability to sense and often anticipate our routine events, we've even started anticipating when our body needs meals without actually hearing those cries. In moderation, this serves well since starvation isn't the path to sanity too; but too much anticipation has caused irregular meal schedules, which has made us lose sense of what comprises us, leading to hormonal dysfunction, and this and that….In short: Absolute Mayhem.

Our body's symphony goes haywire each time we surrender to those 12am Maggie cravings, cravings that as if leave our body worker's face filled with deeply carved contortions. Albeit, they take it all in, without letting a word rumble through our ears. But just like all rubber bands, it too has its breaking point. And when it breaks, it floods us with tears. One cannot fathom how much it is important in providing perfect conditions, away from diseases like Diabetes, obesity…it makes our well-being germinate and thrive.

To heal those untouchable wounds, we do-however- have the magic pill that once fed to our brains could make us act exactly how our body workers want: The hunger scale.

As the name suggests, this scale gives us a once in a life time chance to give back to those workers who sacrifice themselves just to make sure every cell house of the trillions in our body city is working just fine.

It also offers an opportunity to curb diseases like obesity, diabetes, and hence also plays a paramount role in the weight loss journey of anyone. Undoubtedly, this is something I constantly referred back to in my early days and now have formed a Mental picture of the same.

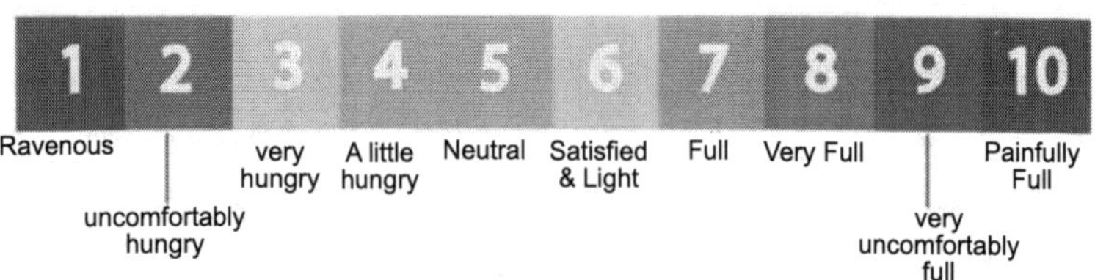

As the figure suggests, the hunger scale is constituted of 10 seemingly blank numbers, but in reality, carries series of emotions and contemplations behind each of them.

Firstly, before learning the hunger scale, it requires a prerequisite: a fixed eating schedule, limited to 3-5 meals, with 5 being the extreme maximum. And no snacking in between the 2 meals.

Just like exercise, having a routine for meal would be a game changer, especially if you're one of those who have late night meal cravings. I have discussed my meal timings in the Q and A section, but first, let's get this done.

Why not snacking? Well, the truth is that our body is world's most complex machine in our universe, which means it doesn't require fuel every other hour or two. It has the capacity to sustain hours without it (in general, having a 3-4 hour window between 2 meals is ideal). And when interfered, it goes into that unproductive mode; the next thing you'd find is the chunks of weight glaring right in your eye.

Having checked this prereq, hunger scale is simple yet requires some deep self contemplation. Firstly, as you prepare to eat your meal, you need to ask your body: How hungry you are. Since our ears aren't capable enough to listen to this most intricate machine, the hunger scale comes to the rescue and acts as a translator. As soon as you finish your last syllable, hold this hunger scale, literally, in front of you and see which number rhymes with the mood, with 1 being ravenous and 10 being a giant's stomach. Ideally you don't want to dwindle off in the range 3-6 but 7 isn't hazardous either.

Once having a number ready, WRITE it down in your diary as time 0. Divide your total meal time in duration of 5 minutes each, and interrogate after every 5 minutes, until you reach the number 6 (The frequency could also be anywhere between 3-6 minutes depending on how long you take. Ideally, you'd want to interrogate at least thrice: start, middle, end).

As drudging as the process sounds, this has its own rewards. For the first week, it'd be a pain to make such efforts, but a pro tip here: If your mind constantly protests at this activity, this has to be the thing to bring breakthrough. Once fluent, everything would be mentally done without needing to write a word (it took me around 3 months to be that proficient).

If facing trouble in the contemplation, here are my 2 cents: usually I could eat about one full pizza when I am either at 1 or 2 (this doesn't happen anymore), so I'd always ask if I can currently eat a full pizza. If no, then the quantity I can eat would help me pick the number up. This way you can also choose any food as a reference which you know can take you from 1-2 to all upto 7-9.

Having hunger scale sorted, there exists another fold of problem: what about false cues? Our mind is notorious to give us false cues, which is nothing else but reminding us to continue to devouring on snacks at odd times to squeeze out fun. But you can outwit yourself by having a planner of the daily calorie goals. There are countless smartphone apps which help you to track the time, the meals you've eaten, and even the calories. Personally, myfitnesspal worked best for me since it not only had the window to scan any packed items and automatically register its name and calories, but also had some calorie estimate of Indian dishes like "Palak Paneer"-based on the quantity- just by entering the name. But as always, the options are endless.

The main goal is that by tracking our meals, we can outwit some of the false cues- usually set off by triggers- by having a broad picture of how our day looks like. And as always, the middle path applies over here as well: avoid the extremes.

Tracking also opens the doors for analyzing if the current diet we've been having is reliable or not, it could require maybe swapping the afternoon meal with morning one, or maybe cutting down on the evening meal's calories due to consistently high ratings on the hunger scale in beginning …In a nutshell: You get to be a scientist! Although this is a tedious, and rather a mundane task, it pays off, as it did for me. Soon, at least in 2-3months, you'd be able to run all these calculations in the head which will stick with you for the lifetime.

Chapter: 6
Triggers

Now that we have established a sense of the things we need to do to lose weight, it's now the time to analyze what leads to the gain in weight. This question might seem simple at first: irregular exercise, overeating, and lack of self-assessment. Let me tell you a similar situation; suppose I come up to you and ask for an address of one particular location in West Delhi and you reply to me "Oh yeah, that's a place in the Asia, probably somewhere towards the southern side." As vague this answer sounds, similarly, the responses I mentioned were also broad and not enough if you want to reach the one particular destination (weight loss).

To know what exactly leads to weight gain, you need to analyze yourself by recording the details in your diary that you must have created earlier to write your goals in. Your task is to figure out environmental triggers that set you off the track. And of course, I am going to discuss some of the most common ones here, but at the end of the day, it's you who has to do it.

One of the Indian TV shows I used to watch was "*Taarak Mehta Ka Ooltah Chashmah*" There is this character called

Dr. *Haathi*, who had a very peculiar hunger level relation: The more stressful he was, the more was his hunger level. What does this tell you? Emotions are one of the most common triggers that set one off the track. Imagine you had a bad day, at school, home, or wherever; the thing that went wrong is just stuck in your brain. You walk over to your snack box, grab a snack, and you start munching…As you take your bites, you are basically not tasting what you were actually eating. You feel refreshed for the short term, but the stress returns, and as soon as it returns, you go and fetch the box, and the cycle repeats. Now in this one process, imagine how many calories you would have already ingested and burned so little of them. If that's you, you need to figure out ways other than eating to overcome such anxiety.

Exercise is considered one of the best busters of all, and its magic lies in the BDNF, discussed in the exercise section. One of its effects, I spoke over there was that it reduces stress levels, and we know exercise increases BDNF. So, more exercise means higher BDNF and hence, lower stress levels. Personally, when I feel like I am not living in the moment due to stress or grogginess, I just jump! I would get out of my chair, drop for a couple of minutes, and then return with boosted attention. And that's exactly what the Nike founder, Phil Knight, used to do back in the days:Run whenever under stress.

Of course, there are other innovative ways to beat the stress even without exercise, one of which is my personal favorite; a power nap! You can plug in the earphones, listen to some soothing music, and just nap for 15 minutes.

Now, if stress is not just the thing that sets you off fetching, another most common trigger is boredom. Imagine one of those days when you are tired sitting at one single place grinding all day for the upcoming test. You can't take it anymore, so you get up and head straight into the kitchen to make a "break". If this sounds like you, then beware of boredom! A study was conducted, which proved that during boredom, one is more likely to switch to unhealthy snacks rather than healthy food. To combat this, one basically needs to have a change in the air. So get out of that chair, switch tasks, or go for a 10-minute walk. Trust me, these techniques will work all the time, and all it requires is the awareness of the existence of these techniques at that very moment.

Do you eat just to get the "required energy" to get the work done? This trigger is one of the most straightforward triggers to deal with. And, all you need to do is get enough sleep...period. As in other cases, exercises can be your lifeguard here as well by increasing the blood circulation in your body, hence making you more awake. Another thing to avoid in these cases is caffeinated beverages. Of course, they really help you to get the work done at that very moment, but they often come with a lot of added sugar. Also, it hinders our sleep, and I have talked more about it in the sleep section.

Now there are some triggers which are basically beyond our control like the birthday parties and weddings we have to attend .As I had mentioned earlier, "Failing to plan is planning to fail." This case can also be handled with well planning. These celebrations are dangerous for those who are aiming to lose weight, so first of all, you need to have a rough idea of numbers of parties you just can't avoid. I am going to throw down some tips which you can incorporate:

1. First and most importantly, don't arrive empty stomached. Eat your regular meals before leaving. Trying to save the calories by fasting will backfire (telling from my personal experience).
2. When you go to the food room, before taking anything, just take a moment to check out all the options available. By doing this, you will make sure you are going for the best possible snack and also sparing yourself some extra time off eating.

3. Don't linger around near the food table. Force yourself to a different corner.
4. Spend more time talking than eating. Have this goal programmed in you that you will be spending time in interacting and meeting new people. Say this aloud to yourself, and watch the magic happen.
5. Watch out for those beverages! Beverages carry out a lot of calories in them, so the best drink is water.
6. And of course, the tips for eating out I had discussed earlier are also applicable here!

And nevertheless, don't forget to "cherish" your favorite food. Because if you don't, you will have an immense regret filled within you, and you might end up eating double the quantity you need. Just watch out for the amount of the food you take at the celebration, and you should be good.

The final and one of the most common triggers I am going to discuss here is sadness. Let me share a story of mine with you. Back in 2009, I met with an accident and was on bed rest for about 6 months. Sad enough, right? Anyone who came in bought chocolates for me. At one point, the doctor told me not to eat any of those since it just kept adding pounds around my belly with absolutely no movement. What I got from this was that we tend to see sadness metaphorically as bitterness, which needs to go away with something sweet. This, in no way, means that people who do this are wrong. Scientifically, the research has shown that low serotonin (a neurotransmitter) levels are linked to depression, and chocolate just brings that level back to normal. So, how to avoid gaining weight while still eating chocolates? Serotonin is secreted by an amino acid called tryptophan, thus increasing the tryptophan levels can automatically help increase serotonin levels (tryptophan is found in food whereas serotonin is not). So firstly, chocolates can be avoided in the first place by eating foods like soy, milk, nuts, spinach, egg, which boosts tryptophan levels.

Another thing you can do is get your body moving. Surround yourself with something that smells good, like scented candles, or even play with a dog. But if nothing seems to work, just make sure before you open your refrigerator, give yourself a 10-minute break. There is a possibility that the urge may pass away. This type of self-control will be a crucial tactic during weight loss and even after weight loss to maintain it.

At this point, you might feel like I sound too repetitive because most of the triggers have similar remedies. The thing to know here is the solutions exist on ONE basal pillar, which can be modified based on the creativity of the individual. I shared some of mine, and I strongly encourage you to make some of your own, which enables you to stick to them more religiously.

Finally, snacks are also sometimes necessary for us, so avoid over-thinking about it. In advance, do some research on the meals you like and choose the ones which has the lowest calories. For myself, I decided 2 Oreo biscuits as my "snack". This had around 100 calories and even if I felt like going for another round, a 200 calorie snack is not that bad once in 2 days.

To sum up, the foundational strategy that can be used in all the triggers is: Eat when you're hungry and stop when you're full. Knowing when to eat and when to stop can be done by the hunger scale, which I had discussed previously.

Chapter: 7

Reduce The Bounciness

Imagine after reaching your goal weight, you take some of the photos of the new you, celebrate it with the people who were there with you, and realize you have traveled a long journey. But after one or two weeks, you just don't feel that good as you felt when you had reached the destination, and as soon as you step on the weighing scale, you realize that you are already on your way back to where you came from! That's the last thing for anyone who has recently lost weight would want to happen. I have heard a lot of cases, from my friends and relatives, of them losing 7 kg of weight, and bouncing back even way higher they came from.

In this section, we will be learning about the chain of events that leads to a relapse and understanding the ways to prevent it.

Temporary failure in following our plans is termed as **a lapse**. Common examples of lapses in the context of fitness training include missing a day's exercise or eating a high-fat dessert.

A relapse is basically the repetition of lapses. Building from above, the examples could be missing exercise for a couple of days for any reason, or eating that good ol' sweet dessert for 3 days in a week.

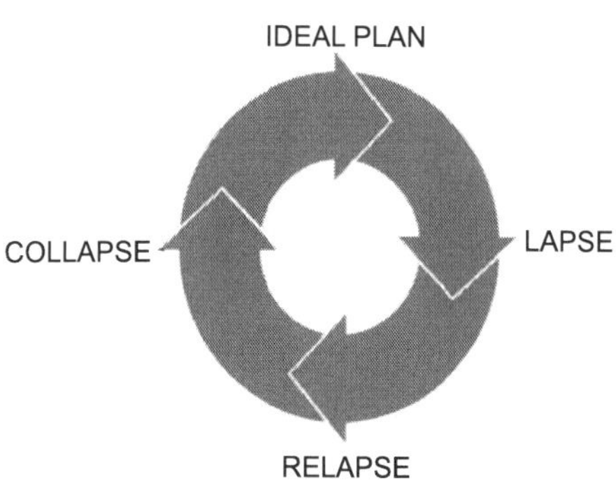

Now, a **collapse** is the extreme version, which means entirely deviating from the fitness plan that had been set earlier for more than a week.

In the above definitions, you might notice some patterns here: each description is getting more severe than the previous. These 3 terms are basically a vicious circle; you fall in one, failure to recover means you fall in the next. For example, failure in completing one day's exercise means you're in lapse. In this case, you have a chance to recover back, but its failure leads you into a relapse. In a relapse, recovery chances are even lower, and finally, failing here leaves in a collapse, which means GAME OVER... This way, you would be gaining back your lost weight, and you may not even realize when you get back to the point from where you had started off.

It is a common misconception that you would never miss out on even a single exercise, nor deviate from your schedule which would prevent you from entering lapses in the first place. But, take my word here: If you go with that mindset, your determination will not last long. Instead, I want you to know that it's absolutely okay to enter lapses because this is something that happens with me as well.

I had pizza, had my all-time favorite Baskin Robbins ice cream, had workout skips because of sick days, etc. But I knew the best way to control yourself is to free yourself a couple of times (remember there's a difference between a couple of times and all the time).

"Shoot for the moon, and even if you miss, you'll end up in stars." This saying is not incorrect and is entirely applicable here as well. Take it this way, you don't have to automatically assume that you have to purposefully miss the exercises or purposefully eat your favourite food just to show that you're aware of lapses. In fact, doing it purposefully wouldn't make it a lapse anymore since it is not something like you are deviating off the path; you're basically digging your own hole for your journey back. All you need to do is to accept the fact that humans make "mistakes" and whenever you do, all you need is to get back AS SOON AS POSSIBLE.

WHAT IF WE ARE ALREADY IN RELAPSE?

Of course, there are some situations when our lapses turn into relapses, and that can't be avoided.

Now, if you start feeling guilty as if you have committed a sin, you would never be able to get out of it, and just go deeper and deeper, hence entirely going off the track. What we see happening over here is the building up of negative emotions stage by stage.

So, one way to avoid entering into relapses is to reduce the negative emotions and have confidence in yourself. For example, for some reason, you happen to miss your workout on Friday, and on Saturday, you go to a birthday party. After coming back from the party, you feel utterly frustrated and start to consider your goals as a doomed failure. And then on Sunday, to reduce frustration (another cue that makes you go off track), you just go out to have your favorite pizza and a cold drink because there's always Monday to get back on your routine. Now, if you take a step back to contemplate what just happened, you could have saved yourself from the over the limit 'Sunday calories' just by having faith in yourself and could have gotten back to your schedule! See, it's that simple!

Still, if the frustration sets in, just have some ways already

ready in your diary that can help you take immediate action like keeping yourself occupied in a puzzle, interacting with someone, etc. And for those of you who think maintaining weight after losing isn't possible, a related research was done in the U.S by National Weight Control Registry, to give your hopes a restart. They tracked all those people who had maintened a weight loss of atleast 30 pounds for atleast a year, and followed them for 10 years. It was found that more than 87% of participants were able to sustain themselves after weight loss through commitment and self-monitoring.

In my case, apart from the usual lapses, for once I even had entered the collapse stage . I had gone for a summer program for 3 weeks. Because of this, I couldn't stick to my workout routines because of the intensity of the program (though, I did go for some short runs) and also had entirely new mouth-watering food options in front of me. After I came back, my jumping stamina came down from that of 20 minutes to 8 minutes. But, I was aware that this happens, and within a week, I was able to come back on my track. And it's going well to this particular day when I am writing this.

Attitude is everything. Another way you can reduce the negative thought influx is by envisioning yourself giving advice to a friend who is stuck in the exact same situation. This technique, if not always, works most of the time; at least it did for me.

Takeaways

1. One size doesn't fit all.
2. Being far sighted while making plans for weight loss is a lot beneficial since losing weight is a gradual process.
3. While setting weight loss goals, constantly reflect of how you felt at a particular point, what comments you received. Emotions are the best motivators.
4. Having someone who keeps you accountable significantly increases the chances of losing weight.
5. Long goals of weight loss must be broken down into steps. For example, in order to lose 20 kg, break your journey in 4 steps by setting new goals at every step. This also opens the door for learning from mistakes.
6. Pro tip: Weigh yourself everyday for best results!
7. When planning out exercises, it's crucial to also plan out for intensity, duration and frequency.
8. For maximum benefits, include mixed intensities of exercises.
9. Have one fixed time for your workouts. Linking workouts with some everyday task significantly decreases the chances of forgetting and reduces the friction to start working out.
10. Have a set strategy for dealing with outings by deciding what you do before, on the spot, and afterwards.
11. Constantly contemplate on triggers that set you off and have a plan on dealing with them. Contemplation is difficult, which is the reason many people fail to lose weight in the first place.
12. Sometimes it's normal to eat the foods we desire the most. Mind the quantity.

13. Having some safe snacks decreases the chances of being caught by those lucrative advertisements.
14. Failing to stick to a plan is normal, but this failure shouldn't be intentional and long term.
15. When in lapse, it's never too late to start building your blocks back again. It's important that you don't just take that as the ultimate defeat and then completely go in that chain reaction of deviation.

Module 5

Q & A SERIES

Diet Related Questions

Q. WHAT DIET DID I FOLLOW WHILE ON CALORIE DIFFERENTIATION PLAN?

Ans. This is another one of the most common questions everyone is looking for. As I discussed in my diet section that I initially started with cutting my calories to 2200 and then went all the way up to 600s, which should be avoided at all costs. For this reason, I am going to provide both, the diet that I followed and the diet that I should have followed, diet information along with the timings.

DIET I FOLLOWED:

1. Protein powdered milk: 11am
2. 2 chilla with vegetable curry 12-12:30 pm
3. Some fruits and Salad: until 4 pm
4. Vegetable curry+more fruits:7pm

And that was it. This is the diet routine I was on towards the end of my journey. In this, I had completely eliminated chapati for at least more than a month and had replaced it with Chilla. I also had brought down my bread and rice intake and instead leaned more towards brown rice. But I am going to repeat again that this detail is superficial since this may not work for someone else. The main key to consider is to analyze your own diet and make some novel recombinations.

WHAT I SHOULD HAVE FOLLOWED:

1. Milk + some light breakfast
2. 2 chapatis + curry + salad
3. 1 chapati + fruits

Q. WHY DO WE AVOID WHITES-RICE, PASTA, AND BREAD?

Ans. Now earlier, I just did that based on the tips I heard in pieces from one way or the other but didn't have any concrete reason. The reason we tend to eliminate white bread and rice is because of its low fiber content. And if you remember the discussion in the diet section about the fiber content, you would know that anything which is low in fiber causes a spike in the insulin release in our blood levels. And so is the case with white bread, pasta, and rice. Since they have low fiber content, the insulin levels suddenly increase, causing the irregular release of insulin secretions, and this causes the blood sugar level to drop below the normal level. You might wonder this should be good since technically we're preventing diabetes right? Not exactly. First off, you want to stay precisely around normal levels to function properly. Secondly, decreased blood sugar levels will make you crave more food and you end up overeating, and regular irregularities in insulin secretion will cause the development of insulin resistance, about which I discussed in the diet chapter.

Q. WHAT WAS MY DIET BEFORE LOSING WEIGHT?

Ans. I have been trying to answer some of the most common questions people have asked me so far, but this is something no one has brought up.Seriously. Even though this diet is something I wasn't very proud of, I chose to write about it so that you can get an idea that controlling your diet is totally possible and can be done gradually regardless of your current intake. The calories I used to intake was…I don't know! Yes, and this is the reason I kept putting on weight in the first place. I would eat anything and everything at any time of the day. I also wouldn't remember what I had for breakfast even after a couple of hours, and instead, I used to take pride in it since Tony Stark from Iron Man 3 also didn't! The only feasible answer I can provide is that on the very first day I started recording on My fitness pal, I was very mindful of what I was eating. By the end of the day, I ended up eating 2338 calories, to be accurate.

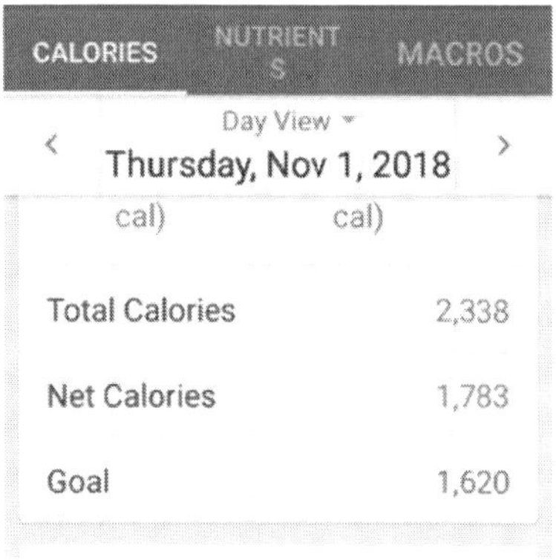

Based on the conversations I have had with my friends who have attempted to lose weight, even they could not recall what they ate a couple of hours ago. So, tracking yourself is the very first step you would want to take when considering cutting down the numbers.

Q. WHAT'S MY DIET AFTER LOSING WEIGHT?

Ans. I have heard of numerous cases where people who lost 8-10kg of weight would end up regaining all of it and in some cases more than what they lost. And I am guessing you wouldn't want yourself to be there. So what changes did I make in my diet after losing weight so that I managed to maintain a constant weight while also overcoming the illness which struck me in the end stages?

Firstly, the biggest mistake people after losing weight make is that they actually end up "unintentionally" falling back into their previous routine and predictably start gaining weight. Of course, as I discussed in my weight loss section, it's absolutely fine to relapse unless you don't make a big deal of it. But in a very structured manner, the next pit they fall into is a severe restriction of calories, which I have discussed endless times is unsustainable. The struggle would continue for a while and then the vicious circle engulfs the innocent's will power, and the person would be seen next day back in his tight fittings.

In my case, after the recovery from illness, I knew I have to change things up since I got so used to that severe calorie-restricted diet. But I was also apprehensive to get back in my previous diet to keep my L sized clothes for the closet itself. I knew I had to figure out a middle path. So, I brought the chapatis back into my diet but with reduced quantity: instead of eating 3 per meal, I started having 2 and occasional 1 per meal as well. Instead of having 1 brunch, I started having breakfast and lunch separately. I also started having proper dinners which included chapatis (I will include a complete list below). But there were some key points I made sure to stick with:

1. I did allow myself to eat occasional chips per week rather than not eating at all.
2. I didn't turn back to sodas at all because of high sugar content.
3. I didn't mind drinking juice occasionally, but I can't really remember the last time I had it as of now.
4. I started eating white rice once in a while but limited pasta. And in terms of bread, I have already switched to wheat bread instead of the white.

This should give you an idea of how small changes in

the diet can be beneficial even when stepping out of the weight-loss cycle. Overall, I reduce the selectivity of my food permeability but never let it approach zero. No matter who's asking, I would still control my sugar intake and absolutely avoid it at night regardless of the circumstance (to prevent inhibition of my growth hormone as I discussed in the sleep pill). Even though I had stopped tracking my calorie intake, I now feel like having an automatic calculator. This automatic calculator lets me know if I am on track throughout the day if the workout I did was ideal (I even realize when I didn't work out enough), and also lets me know if I can break my rule (based on when I last did).

Anyway, here's my diet routine (when I am off from school) right now to the best extent possible:

- Lemon/Green Tea: 8 am
- Banana and Milk: 9:30 am
- Breakfast (could be something light like poha, chilla, or even sandwich): by 11 am
- Lunch (usually 2 chapatis and any vegetable dish): around 2:30 pm
- Intermediate snacks (includes some fruits, salad: usually around 6:40 pm
- Dinner (again, 2 chapatis and any veggie cuisine): by 7:30 pm

* Occasionally, I don't mind eating some chips and chocolates :)

Q. HOW DO I MANAGE MY CHEAT DAYS?

Ans. Cheat days are a key component you'd want to consider while planning to eradicate bad habits. The basic essence of the cheat days is that you follow your non-junk diet on every day except for this one day: The cheat day. As the name says, you allow yourself to eat anything you want which would provide you enough motivation to continue your dieting program until the next cheat day and the cycle goes. But, some people just like the extremes: by eating as if it's the only day of freedom and neutralizing all the pluses they had by their "ideal diets". Then, after 2 weeks, they would stand on the weighing scale again hoping there would be some displacement but seems like nothing ever happened. Dismay sets in, and guess what, they wouldn't even realize the transition to their "good-ol'" diet.

We all want to avoid this situation and see some real-time progress through the displacement of the scale, but we can't afford to skip our cheat days since that's the fuel for our rest of the days. Is there a way out? The middle path rule.

Like I have shown in the past how the Middle path rule works, I am going to apply the same principles over here as well. According to this rule, you shouldn't be consuming all the calories you planned on cheat day on one single day. Rather, it needs to be distributed like the bell curve of the statistics: across multiple days.

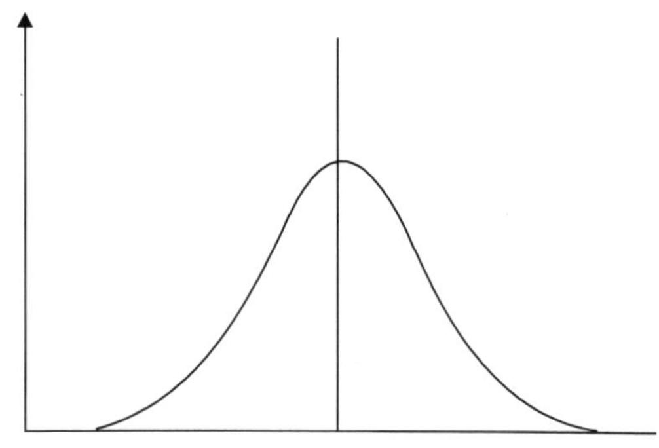

A BELL CURVE

As it is visible in the image above, you need to space out calories to the number of days as much as possible but also to some extent: you also don't want to lose the essence of a cheat day completely.

The way I solved this issue was by keeping only one meal of the day as the "cheat meal" on the cheat day. That meal could be literally anything, ranging from a pizza to a BTW Tikki from a restaurant. For other days, I allowed myself to eat Oreo biscuits on alternative days. And in order to limit my eating from restaurants even further, I went one step further and convinced my parents in investing in air fryer. This way, I was further able to flatten my curve by opening doors to a new variety of food at less calorie intake. In fact, air fryer takes about 50 times less oil than deep frying method to cook pretty much the exact same thing. So, when I said I seldom ate the restaurant food, I really meant it (roughly 3 times throughout my entire journey of about 4 months).

In a nutshell, plan the cuisines you would want to eat on a cheat day, and calculate a rough estimate of the calories. Now at this point, it's on you which dishes you want to spread out and which ones stay for the big day. And if there's some light snack that's very close to you (like the Oreos where in my case), then have a set frequency of intake per week.

*As I mentioned above that using an air fryer can help you cut down the oil and hence make you slimmer. However, it's important to take relativity into account. Air fryer will be better than deep fried method, but still, it's important to keep things in control. Fried foods, in general, can become a big barrier if not taken in moderation, and studies have shown that vegetable oil is linked to increased risk of heart diseases (Coronary heart disease, for instance) and inflammatory responses. Therefore, if you're considering to replace deep fried food with air fried, then good- but also mind the frequency.

Q. HOW TO REDUCE THE IMPACT OF CHEAT DAYS?

Ans. The answer to this is a no brainer, yet I decided to introduce it since I mentioned it in the past question. The best way I used to do it is by increasing the duration of workout. That's it. As I spaced out my food intake, I also spaced out my extra workout durations on those particular days. This way, I knew if I am eating anything extra, I work out extra.

Q. WHAT ABOUT THE IDEA OF WEEKEND BINGING?

Ans. This is similar to the concept of having cheat days, but relatively frequently. As most of us have our weekends off, people on diet also feel like giving themselves a break from their diets on weekends as well. But, I am totally against this analogy. Applying this analogy would make our brain consider our new diet as some sort of a chore it has to do and will be unsustainable.

Q. WHAT ARE MY CHEAT DAYS LIKE AFTER WEIGHT LOSS?

Ans. Cheat days are integral when it comes to losing weight. But, have you ever thought how's the situation afterwards? If you are not interested in regaining the lost weight, this question can provide some support. It's no surprise anymore that weight loss, when done gradually, produces the best outcomes. This also means staying persistent for a longer period. However, for some, once they're done with the "diet plan" they were following, it would stop appealing as it did in the midway.

The key approach to diet, I have talked about over and over, plays a crucial role over here. Those who considered their dieting as a chore, developed the relationship with it as something as of a requirement, would have high temptations to eat out regularly, and soon they could see the displacement of their scale going down.

I never considered dieting as a "requisite".So, I had to

actively make some efforts to again alter my dieting schedule to normal as I did before losing weight. Since I used to keep a track of all my activities, after I reached my goal weight, I never had to do the tracking again. It's all subconscious now. This also means I don't track my cheat days any more as well.

However, I still have a rough idea not to exceed my restaurant food number more than 2 per month. This is no doubt a higher frequency, but now my goal is to maintain weight, not lose it.

Q. WHAT'S MORE IMPORTANT IN CALORIES: QUANTITY OR QUALITY?

Ans. This is another crucial question to remember before starting the journey. For the first 1.5 months at least, I would be consciously eating fruits and salads making sure the trajectory of my weight loss stays negative. But as time passed, I got so obsessed with those stats of calories that I started looking foods as mere calories-choose the one with the least amount of calories, and for this reason, I even minimized my almond intake. By December end, as I discussed earlier, even after I had brought my food number to 500, I didn't bring down my "cheat food" intake by the same proportion. So it is safe to assume that this might also be one of the reasons for the extreme sickness in the post-weight-loss period.

This question is mystical that Christopher Gardner, Ph.D., a professor of medicine at Stanford University, was also interested in exploring this dilemma. He divided 609 overweight adults into 2 groups, one kept on low carb diet and the other on the low-fat diet, for 12 months. Though he found out that the average weight loss was similar amongst 2 groups (11.7 pounds for low fat and 13.2 for low carb), there appeared to be wide differences within the same group. On this, he concluded that "There's no one diet for everyone".

He then followed an alternative approach: the qualitative. In this, he asked both the groups to cut their carb or fat intake respectively, but also consume more satiating foods, more veggies, and cutting down sugar as much as possible. Those who followed this saw a significant drop in the number regardless of the diet they consumed.

Gardner explains, "Steel-cut oats and kale are both low-fat; so are sodas and white bread, but the oats and kale are likely more fulfilling, more satiating. Avocados and nuts are both low-carb; so are lard and butter, but meals made with avocados and nuts may be more filling, more satiating."

The food we eat can have a significant impact on our overall body processes and gene expression. The calories, of, say some almonds and cookies, may be the same for us, but not for our body. And this is precisely the reason why some food groups boost our metabolism. There is no doubt that quantity also does play a role, but finding the right equilibrium between the two is key.

Q. HOW TO NOT KILL YOUR METABOLISM?

Ans. I did talk a little about metabolism earlier, mentioning it's something which is genetically pre-determined and higher the metabolism meaning lesser the fat. But this statement holds true only in certain cases: that is the right environmental conditions as well. From the environment, I don't mean weather or temperature conditions of the area, but the environment you set up for your body by practicing certain habits. I am going to mention about certain habits which tend to disrupt the environment or homeostasis:

1. **SKIPPING BREAKFASTS:** If you remember what I talked in the diet chapter about the "New diet system" workshop I had attended, I mentioned that according to

them, we must eat our first meals, not before 12. But, even though this may have certain benefits, including prolonged intermittent fasting, this does slow your metabolism as it signals our body to be food starvation mode and hence slow metabolism. I tackle this issue by having my dinner at 7 pm and my first meal of the day around 9:30-10 am. But don't forget that even I initially used to eat my brunch at 12 pm but had to stop that due to medical reasons. I have heard many conflicting viewpoints on this case, so the best way to figure out is through experimenting on it on your own.

2. **EATING WRONG FOOD IN BREAKFAST:** Are you one of those who have a junk meal leftover from last night and eat it in the morning to "waste"? If yes, you should stop doing that right away. This is not to say that eating breakfast is some sort of a sacred meal either. Instead, take it this way: a thoughtful start sets up the level for the rest of the day.

3. **Sedentarism:** This is by far the most widespread practice we all follow, including me. It's hard to avoid it unless consciously make some efforts to leave our chair. So, if something seems trivial consciously, the best way is to make it sub-conscious. In the beginning, make some conscious efforts to move around after, let's say, one hour of work. Set reminders. Once you feel like you automatically are inclining towards moving, then that's a good sign.

4. **Avoiding strength training:** The main logic here is that even though the cardio and moderate-intensity workouts do help you burn calories, the effect is not prolonged. High intensity training helps not only burn more calories while in the workout but also ensures calorie burning takes place even after the workout: as long as our muscles repair themselves. Strength training does not necessarily require equipment: it can be anything from skipping to mountain climbers.

5. **Not enough sleep:** As discussed in the sleep chapter, inadequate sleep can very much cause hormonal imbalance- like the growth hormone- and can lead to decreased metabolism.

6. **Stress:** We all have heard that stress isn't good. But I bet none of you saw it coming under metabolism suppressors. The basic analogy I can explain is that stress causes an increase in the cortisol (a hormone) levels which crave us to eat more, exercise less.

Q. HOW TO INCREASE YOUR METABOLISM THROUGH DIET?

Ans. There are numerous ways to increase metabolism by exercising more or increasing intensity. But if you want to have profound effects, there needs to be some stress on the other hemisphere of this world as well. Here are 4 foods that can guarantee you a boost in that metabolism:

1. **High protein Foods:** Whether derived from plant-based or animal-based sources, proteins are hard to digest, thereby boosts the metabolism and hence provides you some automatic calorie reductions from your body. I derive my protein from plant-based sources like protein powder, pulses, etc.

2. **Green and Oolong Tea:** This is something we all MUST be drinking. Not only does it boost your metabolism, but

it also produces phenomenal results. It can back you up for insulin resistance, cognitive decline, Alzheimer's, oxidative stress (contributes to aging), cardiovascular diseases (most common being Coronary Artery Disease caused due to plaque formation), oral health…phew. The list can keep on going but you need to have at least 3-6 cups of tea-green, white (not the milk-based one), black, oolong- to reap all those pluses.

I started drinking tea a couple of months before I actually started losing weight and this, even though didn't cause weight loss due to uncontrolled food intake, helped me maintain a constant weight for months at least.

3. **Coffee:** Now be careful over here. Adequate consumption can help you get that extra boost; however, overconsumption of it can disrupt sleep cycles as discussed in the sleep chapter. And you know the drill: disruption of sleep means an imbalance in hormones and at the end suffers metabolism.

4. **Chilli Pepper:** There's a chemical called Capsaicin which may play a role in burning up those calories. It may be around 50 a day, but hey, if you do some math, it doesn't sound bad in the long run.

Q. WHY DO I STOP LOSING WEIGHT IN THE MIDDLE OF THE JOURNEY EVEN AFTER I AM DOING EVERYTHING RIGHT?

Ans. You have been constantly avoiding the cuisine that melts your heart away, and have been working out even when your body revolts. But, you see some progress through the displacement of the weighing scale, get motivated and just keep going, until you reach a point where…uh, there seems to be something wrong with the weighing scale huh?

This is a very crucial stage since it may be disheartening to have a slower weight loss even though we're doing our exercise and diet things right. Some of you may even throw the towel in. I am going to go over some common mistakes we are prone to make during our journey. And to let you know that you're not someone special here, this phenomenon actually has its own name: Weight loss plateau. Let me explain its mechanism first.

Initially, when we begin calorie restriction, we disrupt our body's homeostasis which makes your body use up the glycogen stores in your body. Since those stores have water as its component, most of the initial weight loss is through that lost water. One evidence for this is that when you start exercising, you notice a lot more sweat initially than in later stages. This was the case for me as well. But this isn't permanent.

Slowly and steadily your body adapts to the deficit calorie intake by in turn lowering the metabolism (this is why it's important for us to make extrinsic efforts to pump it up). This may cause you to have a slower weight loss, but if you stopped losing weight totally, chances are that you slightly went off the path in one of the following cases:

1. Too unrealistic goals: Extreme calorie deficits can be a jetpack in the first month, but when you run out of it, you totally go off. As I have discussed the consequences of extremes in the diet section, this will make you more prone to having cheat days at high frequency or binge eating.
2. Having a strict No List: If you're documenting every step of your weight loss, then good. But if you also have a page of the foods to avoid at all costs, then this may be a problem as well. The issue over here is that if you actually sit down to create a big list, you control your urges, but instead must eat something else of similar harm and be in an illusion of being on track (check out my answer on my big no food list).
3. Jotting out the entire food group: If you remember some of the ideal diet systems I discussed in the diet pill, I mentioned how I wasn't a big fan of the keto diet. This may work for some, but this disrupts our body's homeostasis and can even send someone to the hospital.
4. Monotonous Diet: If you've been following your diet schedule strictly from day 1, and have started to notice some weight loss plateau symptoms, it's time to add create some recombinations to your diet. I dealt with monotonicity by having some flexibility right from the start. In general, we all have a rough sense of which foods to take or avoid, and if not, my fitness pal helped me get some exact stats.
5. Following anyone, or more than one, of the activities that kill your metabolism.

Q. WHAT TO DO WHEN YOUR WEIGHT LOSS RATE STARTS TO DROP OFF FROM WHAT IT WAS INITIALLY?

Ans. I discussed some cases which may lead to plateauing of weight loss in the preceding question, but if you can't relate to any of the cases, I can provide some general tips to conquer this plateau. Firstly, you might need to go through your daily charts to see if you're not ending up having more or prolonged cheat days. Another thing is to increase your workout timings and intensity. When I used to do skipping, I couldn't sustain more than a minute on the first day. I slowly stepped up the game to 10 minutes, even had a sore foot for multiple days, still-after recovery-went further to 20 and 30 minutes. Now, since I can do this particular activity for any duration, I combined another workout-mountain climber and unknown- to still be able to experience the "flow".

Another thing you can do is cut down the calories. However, be ultra careful here: avoid going under 1200. I kept on going and had to face some serious consequences which I have discussed Under the diet section in the minimum calorie intake part.

And if you're still looking for some bonus tips, here's the best I've got: look for opportunities to increase your activity levels when out and about. Derren Brown-English mentalist, illusionist, and author- conducted an experiment in a town where he tested out the difference between folks who claimed themselves to be "lucky" from those who believed they never had enough of luck. He placed a statue of a cute dog on the town's outskirts and spread the word as a "good luck statue" amongst the residents. They observed the activity around the statue, noting who visits it and then tracking their daily activities. His assistants approached those people, disguise as some normal survey conductors, and asked them questions related to luck. Then, Brown secretly kept giving some novel opportunities to both the lucky and unlucky people and figured out interesting phenomena. Opportunities are always available equally to every person, it all depends upon the eye who is able to reap it or not, hence lucky and unlucky. Look around for opportunities to work out: climbing metro stairs, running daily errands.

Q. WHAT WERE THE FOODS ON MY LIST WHICH I WAS SUPPOSED TO AVOID AT ALL COSTS?

Ans. As I raised a point in the past questions about not having a big food boycott list, you must be wondering what I had. I included just 3 items that I had to avoid at any cost: Chips, sodas, and Chapati (apparently). I had a strong addiction to eating chips every single day, and each chips packet had about 500 calories. Had I continued eating this in my weight loss plan, it would have sabotaged my plan completely. About sodas, I learned that they're very rich in sugar as well which might not be a good idea to have if I wanted to lose weight as fast as possible. But this didn't mean I also stopped fruit juices as well (but in diluted form ;)).

For the 3rd item, I am still iffy if I did the right thing or not. As you know, the only thing I wanted to have was losing those cursed pounds encompassing me 24*7. This also meant I stepped in the battlefield without any prep and believed every rumor as a gleam of hope. So the person who earlier ate 3 chapatis a meal had totally replaced it with 2 to 1 chilla per meal! Now if I look back, cutting the number from 3 to 2 and occasional 1 could have worked as well since chapatis are rich in fiber, which means it supports insulin sensitivity.

If you have strong cravings for foods on this list, you can just have a very minute quantity of it and be okay. I did this a lot with my pals where they would be eating chips and I'd just literally take one piece (and that too occasionally) and be satisfied.

Q. WHY IS IT OF IMMENSE IMPORTANCE TO HAVE AS MUCH WATER INTAKE AS POSSIBLE?

Ans. On the onset of my fat to fit journey, as I mentioned numerous times, I was really naive in this subject. And this naiveness also led me to think that more water I drink, more weight I put on. Fortunately, I wasn't very strict about following this rule. Little did I know, there seem to be a plethora of benefits of drinking water.

1. Acts as an appetite suppressor: Have you ever had a big glass of water and felt like not eating anything? Now you know you're not alone. This is why drinking water before the meals can be a hack to lose weight (do note that drinking after eating can cause hindrance in our digestion since it dilutes our digestive juices)
2. Boosts metabolism: I should have mentioned in the question addressing metabolism, but I felt this is something to have a question of its own. Research has shown that drinking cold water has boosted about 25% of metabolism in overweight and obese children. I leave the potentials of hot water on your imagery for now.
3. Necessary to burn fat: Not only water helps in avoiding new fat formations, but it is also a crucial component in one of the steps-hydrolysis-in fat burning process.

I could keep going on, but there's another question: how much water to take in. There's no one size fits all here, but a quick search should help you calculate your personal water need.

The hack I used to solve this was by drinking more hot tea. I used to drink around 2 cups daily and have increased the count to 4 nowadays (due to the current pandemic) which helps to get 2 birds with one stone.

Sleep Related Questions

Q. AT WHAT TIME DO I WAKE UP AND HOW MUCH SLEEP DO I GET?

Ans. This was something I least paid attention to, before I actually learnt about the hormonal play to write in this book. After reading the sleep chapter, it must have provided you a sense of the role sleep has in influencing your well being and hence keeping you motivated to lose weight. Even though I used to sleep for an average of 6 to 7 hours, I never truly had a schedule of waking up and sleeping until now.

If I were to tell you my sleeping schedule while losing weight, I genuinely wouldn't have an answer to that. Though, I have noticed that since I just can't function well under about 6 and a quarter hours, I never compromised in the numbers.

But speaking from a current perspective, after experimenting multiple times with various combinations, I finally figured out the perfect pair: sleeping at 10-10:30 pm till 5-5:15 in the morning. I find myself totally afresh and intrinsically motivated by following this schedule. I have tried sleeping at several different time phases: 11 pm, 12 am, 1, 2, and even 3am (just add 7 hours for the wake up time)! But none of those digits were even close to the charismatic results the former produced.

The best way to figure out your best time is by experimentation. Honestly, after you leave the bed, maintain a journal to record your mental state: are you not willing to leave the bed, are you feeling a sense of enthusiasm to get straight to your work, etc. I did this all mentally but actively.

National Sleep foundation suggests sleeping anytime between 8pm-12pm.Why? This is because of how our chromosomes are coded. Since there happens to be minuscule differences in the human genome, this time range is ideal. However, experimentation is the only key to figure out the optimum stage.

Q. DO I USE ALARM CLOCKS TO WAKE UP AT THE DESIRED TIME?

Ans. Are you one of those you set multiple alarms to just get yourself out of bed? If you are, there's a very high chance that you might not have the best relationship with your alarms. They are so nerve-racking, aren't they?

In the sleep chapter, I suggested how alarm clocks can actually raise our blood pressure levels. But it's also impossible to be without them. So, to prevent the negative effects as well as use those mechanized bird chirps to my benefit, I actually came up with a concrete plan.

Even I used to be one of those who used to set countless alarms each recurring every minute. But it wasn't too late until I figured out the right plan. I knew that having those natural alarms (which have sounds close to that of nature) was the key but having the classical alarm was also crucial. So, I started setting one natural alarm at the time I wanted to leave the bed and 2 classical alarms after it: first one exactly 2 minutes after it and the second one after 10 minutes from the prior. It worked! Not only did it work, but this also made me leave the bed in the span of those 2 minutes to avoid hearing that groggy alarm. Even when I fail to rise on the natural one, the impact of negative consequences is significantly reduced since there's no sudden increase in the alarm volume: thanks to the soothing sound of nature like alarms.

Also, I have also seen myself wake up even before any alarm goes off on a number of days.

Q. WHAT ARE THE TIPS TO BE SYNCHRONIZED WITH OUR GENETIC SLEEP CYCLE?

Ans. In my sleep chapter and even everywhere else, you read that we should be getting around 8 hours of sleep. But to be honest, this is literally just a mean number. You could be on either side of the spectrum. The truth is we all have our circadian rhythm (sleep-wake cycle) embedded in our chromosomes. This means that experimentation is truly the key to solving that mystery. And I didn't find this info on Google, it was from some special place. I actually watched one of the TED talks related to sleep. There, the speaker had discussed all these facts.

The key questions you need to seek answers to while experimenting with a particular duration are- Do you feel groggy, anxious after waking up? Does your overall performance get affected by it? Try one duration period for at least a few days to reduce variability and don't change your current wake up time to keep that variable constant.

As mentioned before, from my personal testing, I found out that if I get even 15 minutes less sleep from my normal duration, I will surely not be satisfied and most likely fall back. Anywhere between 6.5 to 7 hours seems like one of the best durations I could possibly have, but I usually keep it between 6 and 6.5.

Q. CAN WE HAVE SOME CHEAT DAYS IN OUR SLEEP SCHEDULES THE WAY WE HAVE IN OUR DIET?

Ans. As I talk about my sleep schedule, one more important thing is waking up time; I had started waking up around 5:30 in the morning. Now I had this idea of having some break days where, instead of sleeping at 10:30pm, I'd allow myself to stay awake by 11pm and also allow sleeping until 6:30am. Even though things weren't exactly according to plan, I ended up waking at 7:30 or even later which also disrupted my day's schedule. The real problems came when I tried to get "out" of cheat days and follow my regular routine.

I was not only feeling more reluctant to sleep according to the pre-set time, I also had issues in waking up as well. In short, it just disrupts your internal clock and increases anxiety-like symptoms. Instead, stick to what you decide and just accept some "exception" days which are out of your control.

Exercise Related Questions

So now that I have gone through all of the theory and explanations of how you can too instill healthy decisions once and for all, I don't see a better time than now to discuss some of the common questions I have been asked which I might have failed to cover in the chapters. I will also try to come up with some other common questions which I feel like some of you might be having at some point in the journey to your goal. Of course, I have mentioned some of these at some point throughout the chapters, but I feel having them repeated could be

Q. WHAT DID I DO TO LOSE WEIGHT?

Ans. This is by far the most common question people have asked me after they saw my transition. And the answer I would always give to them is in 2 parts: Exercise and Diet. Well, now you know how exercise and diet ACTUALLY MATTER a ton in pretty much every aspect: intellectual capacity, longevity, general well being, efficiency, and whatnot. And you also now know what foods are to avoid and which ones know the best of all. In terms of exercise, it's important to address both the upper body and the lower body exercises. The best exercise in my knowledge which addresses both very efficiently is running.

Q. DID I TAKE ANY PILLS TO LOSE WEIGHT/ WHETHER MY WEIGHT LOSE WAS A CAUSE OF A DISEASE?

Ans. You know, after my board exams were over, it had already been a while since people last saw me. So as I started my regular classes back, whoever would see me would take a while to see if I am the person they think. After conformation, the very first thing they would ask is if everything was alright. Of course, I did not take any pills for the purpose of losing weight. And I didn't lose weight because I fell ill or anything. This was a choice I actively made and worked upon and have managed to maintain myself even almost after a year.

Q. WHAT EXERCISES I DID TO LOSE WEIGHT?

Ans. I focused on specializing in a very small number of exercises: running, skipping, high stepping. In this, my upper, as well as lower muscles, are in play which is what you would want. As I have mentioned earlier, running was one of the major exercises I focused on. The reason I picked up very few but high-intensity exercises were so that I can make myself to exercise pretty much subconsciously rather than something which has to be on my to-do list. Just finished my work? no problem, I would skip for a minute as soon as I get out of my chair naturally. And if I do the same activity multiple times a day, things would add up and I can actually squeeze some bonus workout out apart from my fixed 9 pm workout session (I have this fixed session since November-December 2018 when I started workout).

This in no way means that I didn't explore any other exercises. I also explored a number of different exercises like crunches (including standing bicycle crunches), mountain climbers (this one is another exterminator of body fats), planks, cobra stretches. For reference, the apps form which I learned the different variations of exercises are "Home

Workout-No equipment" and "Six Pack in 30 Days-Abs Workout" which is on both google play store, and app store. To be clear, the sole purpose I used this app was to learn a couple of other new workouts-mountain climbers, high stepping- and make them subconscious: to reduce the expenditure of will power. This is what I'd recommend how the app should be used contrary to following blindly all the activities the app pops up for the day.

Q. "I CAN EXERCISE WITHOUT FAIL FOR THE FIRST COUPLE OF WEEKS BUT THEN IT'S JUST HARD TO FIND TIME FOR IT. WHAT DO I DO?"

Ans. You know that when I started my journey in November 2018, I already knew in my mind this is not the first time. Even so, I had already attempted to lose weight just a couple of months ago by cycling. I checked all the initial items including downloading google fit, setting up goals, "suiting up", and getting my gear ready. I started biking 30 minutes every day with high average speed. And guess what, I faced the same issue. So I must have allowed myself for one daybreak and after that the friction to overcome to get myself back to my bike just skyrocketed.

Most of the folks must be having a similar story. Having high starts, skipping one day of exercise by "rescheduling" the pre-planned cheat day, and then falling into their normal routine. If I analyze my previous situation, I had a wacky foundation. I had not determined a set time which would only and only be for the workout and also didn't link my activity to one of the those hard scribbled activities of my day. Moreover, I didn't have a pre-laid plan, and I never focused on dieting at all.

So you see, not having time is not an excuse. Our ancestors, who lived in an era with no machines never complained of not having time. And paradoxically, we have tons of devices to save time and yet we never have that. Fixing workout time is by far the most important thing to do and linking it to something you usually do around that time just eases the task. In my successful attempt, I had (and still have) the 9 pm time fixed and linked to the favorite show I watch which comes at 9 pm. The show hasn't stopped yet and neither my exercise, making my workout effortless yet enough to fill the floor with 30 sweat drops (yeah, I actually counted those one day). And another evidence that signifies the importance of linking the activity is if I am asked to my 9 pm workouts on Saturdays and Sundays without Aladdin, I just find it a bit hard to do.

Q. HOWMUCHEXERCISEISENOUGHFORADAY?

Ans. To start off, I am going to call this is a very subjective question. I like to do mostly high-intensity workouts since I usually have other commitments (including writing this book:)). The basic concept is exercise should make your heart beat faster. How much faster and for how long is what intensity is all about. By doing high intensity, I can maximize the calories burnt per unit time which helped me stick to my plan in the long term. However, back in 2018, I was a workout fanatic and used to exercise for somewhere between 40-50 minutes a day in total (of course, not in one go). I would have 20 minute skipping session and maybe some intermittent exercising. Doing short sessions instead of one long session prevents fatigue thereby maintaining our intensity and just makes exercise seem a bit easier.

How much you should exercise depends on your calorie intake and how fast you want to lose weight. To provide a rough estimate, it takes around 6.5 hours of cycling at 19-21 km an hour to lose a pound. If you follow your recommended calorie intake and workout for around 25 to 30 minutes in moderate and high intensity, you should be good.

However, don't forget that not to try to over-exercise in your early days of the routine. If you want to exercise more, you're free to do anytime outside the set routine. One of the most common mistakes early exercisers make (even I did when I didn't have a routine months before November and I failed) is that if they have a workout time set, say 6-6:30, they might try to push it up and up with every successive day. While doing this one day or 2 days a week is really beneficial, the long term sustainability is quite low. This is because that if one day you don't feel like working out, you wouldn't be able to cater enough activation energy since your mind would be tricked into thinking that you've already covered today's workout calories in past days. And even the slightest deviation from the routines can lead to collapsing of the entire structure.

One tip I can give you is that you should track your workout exercises (to get an estimate of the intensity) and the minutes you did it per week for a month and observe your weight loss and make changes accordingly.

Q. WHAT WERE THE EXACT CALORIES I BURNT IN MY WORKOUT SESSIONS IN A DAY?

Ans. While my memory of my per day calorie burn has slightly obliterated, fortunately, I do have the recorded data on my fitness pal app (this is why it's paramount to record the sessions). In the very first few days, when I hadn't figured out my central workout activities yet, I started with around 570 calories on the very first day, which predictably started falling in less than 200 in the subsequent days. But, it wasn't too late a see a spike in my activity level, which went somewhere around from 600 and even touched 1000! Until about December-mid in 2018, I see the average calorie burned to be 400-500. However, this average drops to around mid 300s for about a month or so.

So, in total, the overall average calories I burnt may be somewhere in 300s per day. This is because every 20-25 minute jump roping burns around 350 calories, all credits to its vigor, and this was one of the activities which I longed to do the most.

Q. WHAT IS THE SAFE RATE FOR LOSING WEIGHT?

Ans. I mentioned in my last question about keeping track of the rate of your weight loss. But what's the average safe range of the rate you should be in? This is a really important question since this may give you an idea if you're over dieting. The experts say that the magic number is 0.5-1kg per week or 2.5-5 kg per month. There may be slight variation but your main aim should be to stay close to the range. In the month of November 2018, I lost 5 kg of weight (The reason I vividly remember this small detail was because this was one of the rarest moments in my life that I lost some weight). But, I felt like stepping up the game and I then I was aiming for losing 2 kg per week! This was such a big folly and then I faced some extreme consequences which I talked about in the diet section.

Q. "YOU KNOW I HAVE ALREADY READ BOOKS WHICH TALK ABOUT TIPS FOR CREATING NEW HABITS. I IMPLEMENTED THOSE IN MY WORKOUTS BUT THEN I JUST WENT OUT OF THE CYCLE AFTER A COUPLE OF MONTHS. NOW I HAVE ALL THE KNOWLEDGE ABOUT IT BUT I JUST CANT GET MYSELF TO START AGAIN. WHAT DO I DO?"

Ans. This might not be everyone's case, but I know a few who might be stuck in this circle. This seems very natural that having all the info and not able to start off. Considering that you have already tried it once or a couple of times, you might be used to being in the automation mode: working out subconsciously. But the main point to take note of here is that before reaching the automation stage, you have to use your will power to set new goals and make you go back into the field without fail. Another way is slightly changing the reward circuitry a little bit to make it seem like a novel activity. The change could be as small as doing an activity you like only after you do the workout.

You know there have been countless times I have tried to incorporate running as a subconscious activity in the past and even while losing weight. I was able to sustain myself during weight loss by motivation but couldn't keep up the skill. So, in the past week itself, I started running at 5 pm for exactly 30 minutes. I have linked it so that as I come back I can ask about what dinner is and then enjoy the same after an hour or so. These small changes like asking can also make the previously known activity seem novel.

Q. HOW TO MAKE EXERCISING INTERESTING?

Ans. I am not sure how many of you might have this concern, but I definitely had this question before I started my 9 pm exercises. Now, you set out a planner, fix a time, and link your workout with one of your routine tasks. You go ahead and keep workout out without a problem for a month. But now what? If you linked your workouts say for example after you come back from your regular class, you might start feeling a bit monotonous after some time. Even though you would play your favorite music which would pump you up with motivation, it just wouldn't help you sustain it when you're feeling even the slightest low. Even I initially started skipping along with playing some music. As my endurance increased, my skipping time went up from 2 minutes to 22 minutes. But even in a while or so, that music stopped surprising me. I agree I didn't have the golden 9 pm time fixed, but now as I look back, I feel like having a surprising element in workouts is super crucial (I will discuss more on this in the other question).

Anyway, if you want to cherish your workout sessions, consider having something which would be dynamic and you wouldn't know what lays ahead. It may be a random shuffle play on spotify, or even a TV show if you workout at home. The reason I didn't prefer random music plays was because of my peculiar music taste. My music taste is not really defined in a specific genre so it's just hard to predict what music I would enjoy. So, I just don't want the current ones on my golden list to become obsolete.

Now if you happen to workout outdoors and have some similar situation with music as I do, the best thing to do is listen to some videos which interest you. This would not only make your workouts exciting but also help you be a bit more productive of the time. While doing my 5 pm running session, I like to add some the ted talks of the topics that fascinate me. This doesn't require me to look at the screen at all, so I can just play as I go.

Q. WHY IS IT SO ESSENTIAL TO HAVE A SURPRISING ELEMENT IN WORKOUTS?

Ans. In the previous question, I talked about having a surprise element can spice up your exercise. But how? The answer in fact lies in our brain. Human brains are really complex structures which seek novelty in pretty much every aspect of life: to help the survival of the species. Whenever we listen to new music or experience a new stimulus that intrigues us, our brain releases dopamine (a neurotransmitter) which is the reason behind those good feelings. But there's one more thing we complex beings have evolved in response to the repeated stimulus of the same activity: habituation. What this means is that the same song which you felt exhilarating the first time you heard might not appeal your senses that much anymore after listening to it continuously day after day. And in fact, this is what happens with the drug addicts: once they experience a certain level of dopamine release by some amount of drug, they have to keep increasing the quantity of the drug intake to keep up with the dopamine secretion levels.

If you don't know to a certain extent what thing you're about to watch or listen while exercising, you wouldn't have to work too hard to increase the intensity of the thing since your brain wouldn't get a chance to habituate. As I watch the show Aladdin while working out, I do have a idea what the story line is going, but I just don't know what to expect today. This way, my brain does not get habituated to it and I am still having a healthy relationship with it.

Another big benefit of the surprising element is that the curiousness of the surprising element can actually provide the activation energy to make us start exercising which is another major problem faced by the majority.

Q. WHY WORKING OUT WITHOUT ANY STIMULUS FOR 1-2 DAYS A WEEK CAN ACTUALLY ENHANCE OUR PRODUCTIVITY?

Ans. Now, this is something I would have not known had I not started my new 5 pm workouts in which I listen to Ted talks. In one of the talks, I learnt about the increasing digitalization of our era and how our brain is actually rewiring itself in response to that. This had its roots in the fact that nowadays, most parents and students themselves complain about the fact that they can't focus on what they do. But the speaker explains that this is not hereditary and is more of like a consequence of the increased stimulus state by high cell phone usage. He then went on and said this can be corrected by decreasing the increased stimulus state by reducing the cell phone usage.

After listening to this, I thought that if we can do workout for a couple of days a week without any other stimulus, this could be novel in its own self and produce other novel results.

Q. WHAT TO DO WHEN NOT FEELING LIKE WORKING OUT EVEN IF WE HAVE THE ENTIRE PLAN SET?

Ans. Even after having all those thick check marks next to your routine, there will always be one day or the other where you might not feel like working out at all. This situation usually occurs after a couple of months already into the routine. But the solution depends on how long the feeling lasts. If it's just one day, it wouldn't hurt if you slightly bring down a bit or do the job with some breaks in it. However, if you repeatedly find yourself back in the same situation, this would be the cue to spice things up temporarily. Repeated sense of detachment from the routine is a cue that you need to change the way you work out. One way is by switching the frequency of the combination of exercises you used to perform, and the other way out is by including some novel body movements. There are numerous workouts listed on the app I mentioned above. A couple of months ago, even I started feeling just conformable with skipping, and the state of comfort in working out means there needs to be something different. I decided to add high stepping while the ad goes on, and trust me, it is just an entirely different experience.

By just adding these subtle variations, you can rejuvenate your training spirit as well. The only reason I am coming up with different cases when you would not want to work out is that our minds are really creative in forming lame yet persuasive excuses, and I can't stress enough how important is it to keep your body moving regardless of your current state (and even after reaching the goal weight).

Miscellaneous Questions

Q. HOW TO FORM NEW HABITS?

Ans. I never actively learned this process, but after reading the book "The Power of Habit" by Charles Duhigg, there happens to be a paradigm which all of us can exploit for our own benefit. It goes like there are 3 components which lead us to repeatedly performing an activity: cue, the action itself, and the reward. It turns out not much lies in an activity itself that we crave to do it again and again. It is the reward that we crave and the cue acts as a reminder to venture for that award. And that award need not be directly related to the activity and neither does the cue. For instance, the author explained his "unavoidable" habit of eating cookies from his workplace cafeteria. He mentioned that he wanted to lose some pounds and those cookies were acting as a barrier.

The golden way, he explained, was by keeping the cue and the reward constant and pruning away the activity. But to keep those two constant, he actually had to actively identify them first.

He started maintaining a journal where he recorded some specific details whenever he had cravings for the cookies:

Time, other people (if anyone else was around him), item before (the task he was doing before he had cravings), location, and emotion. He kept doing it for a week until he actually started seeing results. He found out that cue was in fact the timing: around 4pm. His brain had rewired to automatically signal him exactly around 4pm to crave cookies. But then he also needed to analyze why those cravings were there: the reward

He analyzed his emotional state journal and found out that it wasn't the hunger he was craving, not even the chocolate itself either, but rather the company of his mates: the conversations. Duhigg then came up with a game plan against his brain: setting an alarm exactly for when he had his cue to get up and converse with his mates. This caused his brain to rewire without any expenditure of will power.

The takeaway here is that almost all the activity's cue can be classified through the key components the author recorded in his journal. If you're curious to read a much more comprehensive study on this matter, I'd recommend you to check out his book.

Q. HOW TO GET BACK ON TRACK AFTER COMING BACK FROM A LONG VACATION?

Ans. Some of us have the opportunity to go to vacations, and when we do, we feel like our body and mind are totally synchronized. We become wide eyed and cherish each new encounter we have in the journey. But even if you don't get to go to your dream destination, most of us at least do get out of our daily cycles for a break. And once we do, we are so much in the harmonic flow of cherishing this new world that our old goals become ultra vulnerable to wearing off. You wouldn't want that, right?

For some, logic may be like just avoiding vacations until we reach the goal weight. But I would be somewhat against it. Agreed that technically you're reducing the chances of contamination of the intricately formed habits, but running away for how long? Obviously, you wouldn't be planning to stay stagnant at one particular place. There will be a time when you move out, and when you do-if not prepared-your weight will follow exponential growth rate. What's worse, you wouldn't even have enough fuel to start from the root one either.

The best way to tackle this is by keeping your eyes wide open for any new opportunity to work out and avoiding as much of those cruel calories as you can. No doubt if you visit a new place which has its own unique cuisine, you will be bound to try it, but also keep your eye open to nab any spark of workout you see in your surroundings. Remember what you started this journey for and carry the journal if you're still losing weight or have some casualties in testing your gut.

In July 2019, I attended a program at Stanford. Since it was July, I was already in shape, had recovered from the after effect illness, and was down to a couple of more pills. By that time, I already had a mental model which would provide me feedback on my calorie gained and burned stats intuitively. As I was traveling, even though I already had planned to get my body moving here and there, I was also slightly worried about the accuracy of my model: if it'd hold true in a country with entierely new dishes as well.

But to my surprise, the feedback I'd get from my body was accurate which also proved that the body feedback I receive is independent of the acquaintance of the food. I didn't stop myself from trying out new cuisines, eating pizza (in moderate quantity), adoring ice cream sandwiches, and even trying out burrito for the first time. But I also made sure that I stay diligent in going for a run every morning-whether with or without my pals- in the campus for around

30 minutes. There was also a decent amount of walking to and from buildings which helped me to walk,give or take, 16,000 steps per day.

I also highly encourage having a mental model set before setting out so that you free yourself from the meticulous work of keeping journals (I discussed how to develop a mental model in the nutrition section in the weight loss section).

Q. WHAT TO DO AFTER WEIGHT LOSS?

Ans. So you worked hard for multiple hours, days, and even months, and when you reach the stage you've been dreaming for all those nights have come.

Cherish that moment.

What you achieved is no less than a life goal for millions out there. Look yourself into the mirror and congratulate yourself for the journey you've led, and thank the ones who have supported you. Enjoy the moment. The enjoyment I am talking about isn't from the facebook, instagram likes; this enjoyment must be intrinsic: for growing more complex than your past self.

Try to think beyond this stage: now what? Not only do you need to venture your next goals to avoid slacking off, you also need to find intrinsic happiness. This will not only keep you mindful of your current state, but also keep you on constant check so that this trophy doesn't slip out of your hands. It's been about 13 months since the day I reached my goal, and I have still managed to maintain it with a minuscule variation in my weight. Though I redesigned my diet, I keep my exercise time of 30 minutes consistent. No doubt that now I never actively think of what I am eating, but staying mindful of yourself in regular intervals lets us know of a fault, if any.

If you're looking for more and in-depth lessons in gaining intrinsic happiness, I can't think of any better book than "Flow" by Mihaly Csikszentmihalyi. I found this a phenomenal book highlighting the human side much more deeply than the genetic side, and the ways of achieving "flow" in anything we do-which can also be applied to weight loss goals.

Q. HOW WILL MY MENTAL HEALTH BE AFFECTED BY FOLLOWING ALL THESE TRICKS AND TIPS AND THE SCIENCE BEHIND ALL THIS?

Ans. Mental health…another buzz word...isn't it? Initially, I had plans to bring this into discussion as well, by exploring the in depth research related to it, but then I settled on the idea on putting this over here. This topic is so dense in itself that it would be just going on its own trajectory; hence I want to keep this thing short.

For having an ideal mental state, you don't really have to make any other efforts. The concept of mental health doesn't exist in isolation, rather it's dynamic and sensitive to our actions to what we do, think, eat, and much more. For instance, BDNF levels increased from exercise act as antidepressants, and certain diets-say Mediterranean diet-have also shown to increase the BDNF levels.

If you're able to follow your workout routines, and don't lose the qualitative aspect of diet, depression, anxiety like symptoms should automatically obliterate. However, if you want to achieve a deeper level of satisfaction and seek happiness in your everyday work, you need some control over what you think (basis of the book "Flow").

In a nutshell, having the balance in our upper hemisphere is paramount, to not to panic when things don't go as foreseen. Instead, experimentation combined with the knowledge in this book, which I tried to wirelessly transfer to your head, should support you maintain order in the consciousness and help balance all the goals you pursue.

Q. IF I WERE ASKED TO LIST ALL THE ACTIVITIES/TASKS THAT WOULD BE NEED TO BE DONE TO BE IN SHAPE-AGAIN- THEN WHAT WOULD IT BE?

Ans. If you feel like you were lost in the specifics of this book, this question should zoom back on the big picture I wanted to convey. I don't recommend following this list blindfolded, but take these pointers as the thick barks and the branches of which I have covered throughout the book.

1. Consider both the components: Exercise and diet. Neglecting either one means no long lasting results.
2. Have a fixed schedule of workouts, and try to keep the deviation in seconds from the chosen time
3. Learn how to expend the least will power possible. Fixing the schedule would do that. This also means working out neither less nor more in ideal conditions (Exceptions do apply when, say, you came back from a vacation, or maybe you increase your workout if you're planning an outing).
4. Linking exercise to some external cue.
5. Constantly making efforts to increase your skills of the workout you perform, by increasing the duration.
6. If you max out the skill, increase the challenges by adding some new exercises and varying their time proportions.
7. Make workouts more enjoyable by linking it to, say, your TV show or watching informational videos. You should also have some no stimuli workouts (if outdoors) to appreciate the nature around.
8. Keep recording your daily performance related to basal components (sleep, exercise, diet): it may be hard to do

such mundane tasks but this is the golden rule.

9. "Failing to plan is planning to fail."
10. Make sure that your indirect factors-sleep, mental health-are well under your control.
11. Keep making new recombinations-be it in diet or exercise or sleep schedule-to maintain that first week spark.
12. Make active and conscious efforts to prune out habits that poke into your goals.
13. Finally, be patient.

Appendix

DIET MODULE

1. https://www.who.int/gho/ncd/risk_factors/unhealthy_diet/en/
2. http://www.strokecenter.org/patients/about-stroke/stroke-statistics/
3. https://www.hsph.harvard.edu/obesity-prevention-source/map-of-global-obesity-trends/
4. https://www.cambridge.org/core/journals/epidemiology-and-psychiatric-sciences/article/making-mental-health-an-integral-part-of-sustainable-development-the-contribution-of-a-social-determinants-framework/3D8A094877CCB42F9051F6277B926683
5. https://www.thelancet.com/journals/lanpsy/article/PIIS2215-0366(16)30024-4/fulltext
6. https://www.worldbank.org/en/topic/mental-health
7. https://www.ncbi.nlm.nih.gov/pubmed/27083119
8. https://www.endocrineweb.com/conditions/hyperglycemia/hyperglycemia-when-your-blood-glucose-level-goes-too-high
9. http://www.attachmax.com/57/postXVII/yoplait-yogurt-nutrition-label.html/yoplait-light-yogurt-nutrition-label-chart-and-template-corner-within-yoplait-yogurt-nutrition-label
10. https://www.nerdfitness.com/blog/everything-you-need-to-know-about-sugar/
11. https://www.medicalnewstoday.com/articles/323818.php
12. https://www.mayoclinic.org/fructose-intolerance/expert-answers/faq-20058097

13. https://sugar.ca/Sugar-Basics/Sources-of-Sugar.aspx
14. https://nutritiondata.self.com/facts/dairy-and-egg-products/69/2
15. https://www.healthline.com/nutrition/is-dairy-bad-or-good#nutrition
16. https://link.springer.com/article/10.1007%2Fs00394-012-0418-1
17. https://www.ncbi.nlm.nih.gov/pubmed/21173413
18. https://www.ncbi.nlm.nih.gov/pmc/articles/PMC3141390/
19. https://www.karger.com/Article/Abstract/325580
20. https://www.ncbi.nlm.nih.gov/pubmed/17921367
21. https://www.ncbi.nlm.nih.gov/pubmed/29494487
22. https://www.ncbi.nlm.nih.gov/pubmed/20071648
23. https://annals.org/aim/article-abstract/1846638/association-dietary-circulating-supplement-fatty-acids-coronary-risk-systematic-review
24. https://onlinelibrary.wiley.com/doi/full/10.1111/1541-4337.12011
25. https://www.ncbi.nlm.nih.gov/pubmed/20463040
26. https://www.ncbi.nlm.nih.gov/pubmed/19457271
27. https://www.healthline.com/nutrition/is-dairy-bad-or-good#acne-and-cancer
28. https://www.medicinenet.com/script/main/art.asp?articlekey=168545
29. https://www.healthline.com/nutrition/healthy-low-fat-foods#section1
30. https://www.medicalnewstoday.com/articles/323818.php#fructose-vs-glucose

31. https://www.healthline.com/nutrition/is-fruit-good-or-bad-for-your-health#section3
32. https://www.healthline.com/nutrition/20-foods-with-high-fructose-corn-syrup#section18
33. https://www.healthline.com/nutrition/9-signs-and-symptoms-of-ibs
34. https://blog.biostarus.com/lassi/
35. https://www.insider.com/whats-the-big-deal-about-greek-yogurt-2018-11#regular-yogurt-has-higher-levels-of-calcium-and-other-important-nutrients-6
36. https://www.medicalnewstoday.com/articles/295714.php#types
37. https://www.healthline.com/nutrition/7-benefits-of-yogurt
38. https://www.healthline.com/nutrition/9-signs-and-symptoms-of-ibs
39. https://www.medicalnewstoday.com/articles/295714.php#types
40. https://livewell.jillianmichaels.com/disadvantages-yogurt-5453.html
41. https://edition.cnn.com/2015/07/27/health/frozen-yogurt-versus-ice-cream/index.html
42. https://www.ncbi.nlm.nih.gov/pubmed/17617461
43. https://www.ncbi.nlm.nih.gov/pubmed/24862170
44. https://www.ncbi.nlm.nih.gov/pubmed/12324283
45. https://www.ncbi.nlm.nih.gov/pubmed/16280432
46. https://www.ncbi.nlm.nih.gov/pubmed/19007893/
47. https://www.ncbi.nlm.nih.gov/pubmed/3200909
48. https://www.livestrong.com/article/531926-does-a-diet-soda-affect-insulin/

49. https://www.huffpost.com/entry/diet-soda-psychology_n_5785586
50. https://www.healthline.com/nutrition/diet-soda-good-or-bad
51. https://www.healthline.com/nutrition/artificial-sweeteners-good-or-bad#cancer
52. https://www.nejm.org/doi/full/10.1056/NEJMsa1504267
53. https://www.health.harvard.edu/staying-healthy/do-you-need-a-daily-supplement
54. https://vascularcures.org/what-is-vascular-disease/
55. https://www.health.harvard.edu/blog/harmful-effects-of-supplements-can-send-you-to-the-emergency-department-201510158434
56. https://www.healthline.com/health/do-you-need-take-vitamins#risks
57. https://www.medicalnewstoday.com/articles/324863
58. https://www.mayoclinic.org/diseases-conditions/parkinsons-disease/symptoms-causes/syc-20376055
59. https://www.healthline.com/nutrition/cooking-nutrient-content#bottom-line
60. https://www.ncbi.nlm.nih.gov/pmc/articles/PMC3673773/
61. https://www.ncbi.nlm.nih.gov/pubmed/3984927
62. https://www.ncbi.nlm.nih.gov/pubmed/24092765
63. https://www.ncbi.nlm.nih.gov/pubmed/12106620
64. https://www.ncbi.nlm.nih.gov/pubmed/25178568
65. https://www.ncbi.nlm.nih.gov/pubmed/15148063
66. https://www.nap.edu/read/11537/chapter/17
67. https://www.nap.edu/read/11537/chapter/32

68. https://www.nap.edu/read/11537/chapter/38#342
69. https://www.fasebj.org/doi/abs/10.1096/fasebj.28.1_supplement.40.4
70. https://www.healthline.com/nutrition/calorie-restriction-risks#section7
71. https://www.medicalnewstoday.com/articles/325745#How-caloric-restriction-aids-metabolic-health
72. https://www.thorne.com/take-5-daily/article/what-effect-does-calorie-restriction-have-on-the-brain

EXERCISE MODULE

1. https://www.slideshare.net/AshleyKoeppen/history-of-physical-fitness-in-asian-culture-72719736
2. https://www.artofmanliness.com/articles/the-history-of-physical-fitness/
3. https://www.artofmanliness.com/articles/a-primer-on-movnat/
4. https://www.medicalnewstoday.com/articles/latest-evidence-on-obesity-and-covid-19#Why-is-obesity-a-risk-factor?
5. https://www.health.harvard.edu/staying-healthy/how-to-boost-your-immune-system
6. https://www.who.int/dietphysicalactivity/physical-activity-recommendations-18-64years.pdf
7. https://www.moneycontrol.com/news/trends/current-affairs-trends/more-than-50-indians-are-physically-inactive-less-than-10-engage-in-recreational-physical-activity-report-2582771.html
8. https://www.timesnownews.com/health/article/35-per-

cent-of-indians-are-insufficiently-active-what-does-it-mean-for-india/286376

9. https://www.who.int/mediacentre/news/releases/release23/en/
10. https://en.wikipedia.org/wiki/High-intensity_interval_training
11. https://health.clevelandclinic.org/exercise-and-your-glucose-levels-does-timing-make-a-difference/
12. https://www.mayoclinic.org/healthy-lifestyle/stress-management/in-depth/stress/art-20046037
13. https://www.todaysdietitian.com/newarchives/111609p38.shtml
14. https://www.diabetes.co.uk/body/glucagon.html
15. https://www.diabetesselfmanagement.com/managing-diabetes/treatment-approaches/increasing-insulin-sensitivity/
16. https://www.healthline.com/health/mental-health/serotonin#functions
17. https://www.naturalstacks.com/blogs/news/76618565-why-bdnf-is-miracle-gro-for-your-brain
18. https://www.technogym.com/int/newsroom/hirt-home-gym-workouts/
19. https://en.wiktionary.org/wiki/neuritogenesis
20. https://www.alz.org/alzheimers-dementia/what-is-alzheimers
21. https://elifesciences.org/articles/15092
22. http:/yoga.org.nz/what-is-yoga/yoga_definition.htm
23. https://www.urbanpro.com/a/yoga-india-popular-yoga-forms
24. http://www.healthofchildren.com/U-Z/Yoga.html

25. https://osteopathic.org/what-is-osteopathic-medicine/benefits-of-yoga/
26. https://nccih.nih.gov/health/yoga/introduction.htm
27. https://en.wikipedia.org/wiki/Visual_cortex
28. https://study.com/academy/lesson/parietal-lobe-definition-functions-quiz.html
29. http://www.ulifeline.org/articles/450-good-stress-bad-stress
30. https://www.mayoclinic.org/diseases-conditions/post-traumatic-stress-disorder/symptoms-causes/syc-20355967
31. https://economictimes.indiatimes.com/magazines/panache/suffering-from-migraine-its-a-neurological-disorder/articleshow/65717851.cms
32. https://www.healthline.com/nutrition/13-benefits-of-yoga#section12
33. https://en.wikipedia.org/wiki/Bikram_Yoga
34. Apple Dictionary definition- Bikram Yoga
35. https://www.vox.com/2015/7/22/9012075/yoga-health-benefits-exercise-science
36. https://www.ncbi.nlm.nih.gov/pubmed/16979397
37. https://www.ncbi.nlm.nih.gov/pubmed/12039436
38. https://www.ncbi.nlm.nih.gov/pmc/articles/PMC2821174/
39. https://www.cambridge.org/core/journals/psychological-medicine/article/research-letter-brainderived-neurotrophic-factor-in-romantic-attachment/97DE2ED50FFC327CDC0CD1B49C33D3BD
40. https://selfhacked.com/blog/a-comprehensive-list-of-

natural-ways-to-increase-bdnf/#DietFoods_to_Increase_BDNF

41. https://www.ncbi.nlm.nih.gov/pubmed/24687840
42. https://en.wikipedia.org/wiki/Homeostasis
43. https://en.wikipedia.org/wiki/Aerobic_exercise
44. https://en.wikipedia.org/wiki/Anaerobic_exercise
45. https://en.wikipedia.org/wiki/Endurance_training
46. https://www.t-nation.com/training/tip-surprising-new-research-on-rep-ranges
47. https://journals.plos.org/plosone/article?id=10.1371/journal.pone.0012033
48. https://www.jackedfactory.com/the-truth-about-rep-ranges/
49. Research on how important is to balance the rep cycles- https://journals.plos.org/plosone/article?id=10.1371/journal.pone.0012033
50. https://en.wikipedia.org/wiki/Skeletal_muscle
51. https://d3c33hcgiwev3.cloudfront.net/_26b3ee3c4db6a2f8af4911a5cc18ff7e_ACSM-High-Intensity-Interval-Training.pdf?Expires=1568764800&Signature=Tv1r4lwJpyaF8KHOTMdgBuBqEzf~WquvtoqmfwTe1QloIiw74UGHE~8P7SrWEEgIHLpP4B4-Wo9Ov-yHLB~ciFHsaakJtCjkvdt9HwdtXt4bEkMmXrUcDIB1rF4ldkomt4KpLUd8i7QE3peAJ-0ZVFVbAcjVSnlWwSHXeEXKldg_&Key-Pair-Id=APKAJLTNE6QMUY6HBC5A
52. https://blog.myfitnesspal.com/how-much-weight-is-safe-to-lose-in-a-month/?otm_medium=onespot&otm_source=onsite&otm_content=homepage:homepage-header-unit&otm_click_id=undefined

COURSES DONE

1. Biohacking your brain's health by Emory University
2. Stanford introduction to food and health by Stanford university
3. Designing your personal weight loss plan by case western university

SLEEP MODULE

1. http://healthysleep.med.harvard.edu/interactive/timeline
2. http://healthysleep.med.harvard.edu/healthy/matters/history
3. https://www.popsci.com/blog-network/our-modern-plagues/do-microbes-sleep/
4. https://www.nigms.nih.gov/education/fact-sheets/Pages/circadian-rhythms.aspx
5. https://journals.plos.org/plosone/article?id=10.1371/journal.pone.0150929
6. https://www.ncbi.nlm.nih.gov/pubmed/1947596
7. https://www.ncbi.nlm.nih.gov/pubmed/6866101
8. https://www.ncbi.nlm.nih.gov/books/NBK19956/
9. https://www.psychologytoday.com/us/blog/dream-factory/201805/more-evidence-dreams-reflect-learning-during-sleep
10. https://www.scientificamerican.com/article/the-science-behind-dreaming/
11. http://learnmem.cshlp.org/content/19/7/264.full.html#ref-30
12. https://www.researchgate.net/publication/311269232_NREM_sleep_spindles_are_associated_with_dream_recall

13. https://www.ncbi.nlm.nih.gov/pmc/articles/PMC3065172/pdf/nihms-280752.pdf
14. https://evolution-institute.org/do-we-sleep-better-than-our-ancestors-how-natural-selection-and-modern-life-have-shaped-human-sleep/
15. https://www.alaskasleep.com/blog/tips-creating-ideal-sleep-environment
16. https://www.nbcnews.com/better/health/how-what-you-eat-affects-how-you-sleep-ncna805256
17. https://www.sciencedirect.com/topics/neuroscience/suprachiasmatic-nucleus
18. http://healthysleep.med.harvard.edu/healthy/matters/benefits-of-sleep/learning-memory
19. https://www.tuck.com/sleep-hgh/
20. Research paper for learning and REM sleep- http://citeseerx.ist.psu.edu/viewdoc/download?doi=10.1.1.891.3079&rep=rep1&type=pdf
21. Research paper for sleep and phone use- https://www.ncbi.nlm.nih.gov/pmc/articles/PMC4089837/
22. https://www.tuck.com/sleep-hygiene/
23. https://www.scienceabc.com/humans/soft-drinks-like-coca-cola-mountain-dew-contain-caffeine.html
24. https://www.sleepfoundation.org/articles/caffeine-and-sleep
25. https://mainehealth.org/services/autoimmune-diseases-rheumatology/inflammatory-diseases
26. https://www.cdc.gov/sleep/about_sleep/chronic_disease.html
27. https://www.medicaldaily.com/lack-sleep-inflammatory-diseases-arthritis-periodontis-cancer-391321
28. https://www.forbes.com/sites/quora/2017/06/20/what-

happens-to-your-body-if-you-get-fewer-than-six-hours-of-sleep-every-night/#4915ab4e3932

29. https://www.yourgenome.org/facts/what-is-a-telomere
30. Research paper for telomere length and sleep- https://journals.plos.org/plosone/article?id=10.1371%2Fjournal.pone.0047292#pone.0047292-Prather1
31. Research paper for telomere and sleep in women- https://journals.plos.org/plosone/article?id=10.1371/journal.pone.0023462
32. https://www.ninds.nih.gov/Disorders/Patient-Caregiver-Education/Fact-Sheets/Restless-Legs-Syndrome-Fact-Sheet
33. https://www.tuck.com/neurotransmitters/
34. https://www.eurekalert.org/pub_releases/2012-06/plos-tro061412.php
35. https://www.webmd.com/sleep-disorders/muscle-relaxation-for-stress-insomnia
36. http://europepmc.org/abstract/med/24576855
37. https://www.webmd.com/pain-management/what-is-the-placebo-effect#1
38. https://journals.lww.com/acsm-msse/Fulltext/2010/05000/Fitness_and_Exercise_as_Correlates_of_Sleep.8.aspx
39. https://www.ncbi.nlm.nih.gov/pubmed/17644426
40. https://www.tuck.com/exercise-and-sleep/
41. Research on timings of exercise- https://news.feinberg.northwestern.edu/2016/10/muscles-have-circadian-clocks-that-control-exercise-response/
42. https://blog.myfitnesspal.com/circadian-clock-affects-workout-time/

43. https://blog.myfitnesspal.com/should-you-get-an-extra-hour-of-sleep-or-a-workout/?utm_source=international&utm_medium=email&utm_campaign=MFP_Intl_NL_UI_Weekly_2019603&os_ehash=55@sfmc:191523033
44. https://www.researchgate.net/publication/281434319_Caffeine_and_Sleep_in_Adolescents_A_Systematic_Review
45. https://www.ncbi.nlm.nih.gov/pmc/articles/PMC3427038/
46. https://www.tuck.com/insomnia/
47. https://onlinelibrary.wiley.com/doi/full/10.1111/jsr.12323
48. https://www.tuck.com/stages/
49. https://www.tuck.com/sleep-inertia/
50. https://www.dailymail.co.uk/health/article-412283/How-alarming-Your-bedside-clock-bad-health.html
51. https://sites.psu.edu/siowfa15/2015/09/16/is-your-alarm-clock-bad-for-your-health/

WEIGHT LOSS MODULE

1. https://www.desiblitz.com/content/calories-and-indian-food
2. https://journals.plos.org/plosone/article?id=10.1371/journal.pone.0031027
3. https://www.ncbi.nlm.nih.gov/pmc/articles/PMC4381486/
4. https://www.medicalnewstoday.com/kc/serotonin-facts-232248
5. https://www.verywellmind.com/why-do-i-crave-carbs-1065212
6. https://www.medicalnewstoday.com/articles/322416.php

7. https://d3c33hcgiwev3.cloudfront.net/_a80fe9a-be45675799614226c 085a83c0_MOOC---Behaviors-for-sucessful-weight-loss.pf?Expires=1569369600&Signature=Qd7QKFob123b3qt-x8hsIGnG1F9lDxrUmSwmeYN2Q-BBqtCQiGT4aSHPRM~Pl1mIW~IvTHF2KvjiBOTE99Zi2LWNaxYXMKxJ-1xyY4xugMB-s1kEmLuMBBThl7HYh1Led5LagzZ-Bx7mI2Fm-jkG7WFC6X030C3-slL7xXG6NpbBU_&Key-Pair-Id=APKAJLTNE6QMUY6HBC5A

FOR THE Q AND AS

1. https://www.verywellfit.com/how-much-exercise-to-lose-weight-3495493
2. https://www.psychologytoday.com/us/blog/the-athletes-way/201711/neuroscience-reveals-why-favorite-songs-make-us-feel-so-good
3. https://www.ncbi.nlm.nih.gov/pubmed/27818336
4. https://www.ncbi.nlm.nih.gov/pubmed/21118617
5. https://www.healthline.com/nutrition/air-fryer#section3
6. https://blog.myfitnesspal.com/8-bad-habits-that-kill-your-metabolism/? utm_source=mfp&utm_medium=email&utm_campaign=MFP_Extra_Metabolism_2020311_INTL
7. https://www.mindbodygreen.com/0-17286/9-surprising-health-benefits-of-drinking-tea.html
8. https://blog.myfitnesspal.com/add-these-metabolism-boosting-foods-to-your-diet/?utm_source=mfp&utm_medium=email&utm_campaign=MFP_Extra_Metabolism_2020311_INTL
9. https://www.nbcnews.com/better/health/i-m-doing-everything-right-i-m-still-not-losing-ncna866376

10. https://www.mayoclinic.org/healthy-lifestyle/weight-loss/in-depth/weight-loss-plateau/art-20044615
11. https://www.ncbi.nlm.nih.gov/pubmed/16822824
12. https://www.healthline.com/nutrition/drinking-water-helps-with-weight-loss#section5
13. https://www.medicalnewstoday.com/articles/322296#how-much-water-do-you-need-to-drink
14. https://blog.myfitnesspal.com/quality-of-calories-more-important-than-quantity/

DIET MODULE IMAGE

1. World obesity chart: https://www.hsph.harvard.edu/obesity-prevention-source/map-of-global-obesity-trends/
2. Ch2, carbs as devil: https://pixabay.com/illustrations/satan-devil-symbol-red-cartoon-2115277/
3. Insulin resistance lock and key: https://www.publicdomainpictures.net/en/view-image.php?image=290577&picture=money-key&__cf_chl_jschl_tk__=b07008ce359007ffc65cf9c34a32
   3c 05a05fcb0-1596384566-0-AWx5jj3YE9wPb-
   hQTTpzobgcdkAulQbbfQMmMxVHvDNRPsBOO
   nHEMm7nEQyjuPCvLHv8kRYtWSeHua-VeeCLviVh-
   c5x4m-Gj966g
   PFZQVkNEc0RMQilAjBEotTx_AtPqUuK7CDAg-
   r3EmSDClTWL0Z3NR1muUPiK5RGYKUyVi5JY-
   q2zD0oDwvbplFaMiQqoky4gTEQOJPX9HdA_l6tU
   aWukMGCIt74wlOlQRxr45wJ6kOT0U6U_6cHq0AI
   schXVzKd7M_lntx8-fPB5wK-yJ9zcgFae42szdRedJjI-
   uUqneU9qnngtgicdxcIerNPOMue5bh-S8qAUO1UX-
   DDA61m7lcHwPFTUSsQDmp6LzWlENnux5h-

WXKNjQWkwpsdvLKsgz6dn6-QTL9ugq2wf-nm0B2-Ao

4. Fat types ch 4
5. Ch5, french fries: https://www.needpix.com/photo/856709/cartoon-chips -character-characters-cute-fast-food-food-french-fries-fries-fun
6. Ch5, potato: https://pixabay.com/get/53e0d64a435ba914 ead98274c02f3e 771622dfe05a5772417d2672d2.svg?attachment=
7. Ch5, veggies: https://www.needpix.com/photo/download/950203/ veggies-vegetables-healthy-food-fresh-vegetarian-organic-green-nutrition
8. Ch5, junk burger: https://pixabay.com/illustrations/fastfood-hamburger -food-3419958/
9. Ch5, pizza:https://pixabay.com/vectors/pizza-mascot-character-cartoon -4665131/
10. Ch6, labels: https://www.flickr.com/photos/theimpulsivebuy/14195290619
11. Ch6, kefir: https://commons.wikimedia.org/wiki/File:Beneficio-do-kefir.jpg
12. Ch8, candiesas sugar addict: https://svgsilh.com image/312222.html
13. Ch8, another candy: https://svgsilh.com/image/575432.html
14. Ch10 , pills: https://www.needpix.com/photo/download/171741/ medicine-bottle-pills-medication-free-vector-graphics-free-pictures-free-

photos-free-images-royalty-free

15. Ch11, Food pyramid : https://pixabay.com/images/download/food-pyramid-5329204.svg?attachment
16. Ch11, Intermittent fasting: https://www.flickr.com/photos/182229932@N07/48655008176
17. Ch12, baby food: https://www.publicdomainpictures.net/en/view-image.php?image=182497&picture=baby-stuff-26&__cf_chl_jschl_tk__=a9e7888d0fc734ffb9554bc98fb10224e610ac57-1596396142-0-AYhYmyFzBmlss-HO94OYs8eBGFC4ORMWTOWMkFjm7iXxhF9R-GW3nIMkQW4NR1ovdtIL-igU0l3L2Ogq1kmb4Yi-v81CjgMWooejIaog9iZaBrnUE87W5s84dn8IiO-ZGyHeyB8UiHF6VpGa4T_DfmSF1OKwrXr7nk-k3fEedTZHSepuwHjEJfodWphkmsJBGBKuxJoGVh-WPnDxx6aJ7dV1K8JHmo639Qlc4pngmGf9Rq8n-lIdsV_I6DTMyS0Kqy_kGDDg9bDOaRDyDE6f2BNxKYBRri_3mN24jUoh0Lv4PwlwcuRgLX0sFE_Jckv7yo-SOI0Wl-5ILhE9e7ftX2-da8bZ9xtxCDcaZ1plAyMM6-yQeBp9b4CSQ83ybDIGtPWImTd4n--riMtAhTBNu-fUWlyJI

EXERCISE MODULE IMAGES

1. (ch8)Exercises in human face: https://freesvg.org/fitness-head-profile
2. (2)ATP dollar bill: https://freesvg.org/dollar-banknotes-vector-image
3. Ch3, person lifting weights: https://svgsilh.com/image/293955.html
4. ch3, lungs : https://pixabay.com/illustrations/lungs-lung-icon-respiration-2803208/
5. Ch3, heart exercising: https://freesvg.org/

download/62794

6. Ch4 brain smart: https://www.needpix.com/photo/download/1147284/brain-clever-thought-dear-hats-intelligence-clipart-cartoon-kids
7. Ch4, neurons as tress: https://pixabay.com/vectors/plant-silhouette-grey-tree-leaves-312737/
8. Ch5, no to sugar: https://pixabay.com/illustrations/cartoon-donuts-donut-chocolate-4764725/
9. Ch6, well being,added after well being: https://pxhere.com/en/photo/1447197
10. See saws on ch 9
11. Oxygen carriers ch9, after the word oxygen carriers in performance enhancers.
12. Ch10, exercise as pill: https://pixabay.com/vectors/medicine-pills-pharmaceuticals-294092/
13. Plaque formation ch10: https://commons.wikimedia.org/wiki/File:2113ab_Atherosclerosis.jpg
14. https://www.123rf.com/photo_68743165_stock-vector-atherosclerosis-stages-disturbance-of-lipid-and-protein-metabolismadjournment-the-cholesterol-plaqu.html

SLEEP MODULE IMAGES

1. Person sleeping peacefully: https://freesvg.org/vector-illustration-of-person-sleeping
2. Unproductivity: https://commons.wikimedia.org/wiki/File:A_Cartoon_Man_Sleeping_At_Work.svg
3. Watery eyes:https://www.goodfreephotos.com/public-domain-images/sleepless-eyeballs-vector-clipart.png.php
4. Power button: https://freesvg.org/power-on-button-symbol
5. Sleep cycle : https://publicdomainvectors.org/en/free-clipart/Vector-illustration-of-the-24-hour-lightdark-

cycle/5460.html

6. Recommended sleep: https://commons.wikimedia.org/wiki/File:NSF_Sleep_Duration_Recommendations_Chart.jpg
7. Brain : https://www.pxfuel.com/en/free-photo-osjki
8. Brain lifting dumbbell: https://www.needpix.com/photo/596605/brain-growth-learning-mindset-school-train
9. Learning new things: https://commons.wikimedia.org/wiki/File:Active_Learning_(27461)_-_The_Noun_Project.svg
10. Idea mind: https://pixabay.com/get/52e0d0414356aa14ead98274c02f3e771622dfe05a57734f722c7fd0.png?attachment=
11. Junk food insomnia: https://www.needpix.com/photo/download/1219453/colorful-doodle-soda-cartoon-set-fries-fast-eat-unhealthy-pop
12. Alarm clock: https://www.goodfreephotos.com/vector-images/alarm-clock-vector-graphic.png.php
13. Person exercising: https://pixabay.com/get/54e9d64a4f57b114f6de8d7ac0213e7d083edbec5553774075267a.svg?attachment=
14. Caffeine addict: https://freesvg.org/download/168815
15. Telomere eyes: https://www.needpix.com/photo/download/96707/eyes-watching-cartoon-pupils-free-vector-graphics-free-pictures-free-photos-free-images-royalty-free
16. Old man glasses: https://freesvg.org/older-person-icon
17. Sleep spindles:https://commons.wikimedia.org/wiki/File:Stage2sleep.svg

WEIGHT LOSS MODULE IMAGES

1. (ch1)SMART goals: https://commons.wikimedia.org/wiki/File:SMART-goals.png
2. Weighing scale: https://pixabay.com/vectors/scale-machine-weight-weighing-37772/
3. T shirt: https://svgsilh.com/image/1093333.html
4. (ch4)Planning is key: https://pixabay.com/get/55e9d5454d5bad14ead98274c02f3e771622dfe05a57724d71277ad7.jpg?attachment=
5. (ch7) Cycle loop: https://svgsilh.com/607d8b/image/2019530.html

Before

After

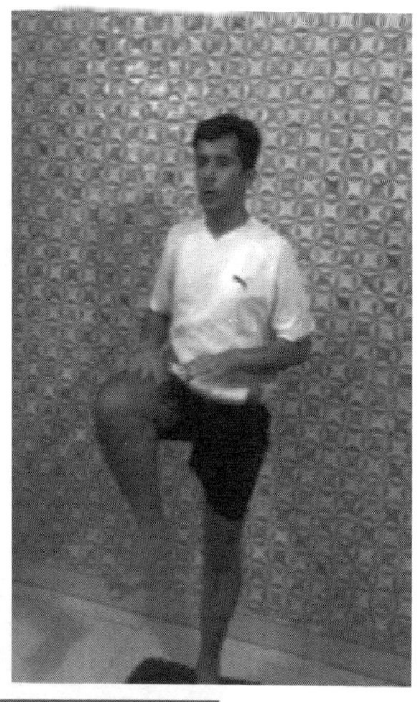

Childhood Accolades